DOCTOR'S ORDERS

*A Guide for Helping Modern Women
Reclaim Their Femininity for Good*

By
Keli Pitts
"The Femininity Doctor"

Doctor's Orders

A Guide for Helping Modern Women Reclaim Their Femininity for Good

Copyright © 2021 Keli Pitts "The Femininity Doctor"
Printed in the United States of America

All rights reserved. No part of this publication may be reproduced, distributed, or transmitted in any form or by any means, including photocopying, recording, or other electronic or mechanical methods, without the prior written permission of the publisher, except in the case of brief quotations embodied in critical reviews and certain other noncommercial uses permitted by copyright law. For permission requests, write to the publisher, addressed Attention: Permissions Coordinator at: info@abundantpress.com.

Ordering Information & Quantity Sales: Special discounts are available on quantity purchases by corporations, associations, and others. For details, contact the publisher. Orders by U.S. & International trade bookstores and wholesalers at: info@abundantpress.com. Printed in the United States of America- Library of Congress-in-Publication Data.

First Edition, First Printing 2-14-2021   ISBN: 978-1-948287-24-1

Disclaimer

The information within this book is intended as reference material only and not as medical or professional advice. Information contained herein is intended to give you the tools to make informed decisions about your wellness, lifestyle, and physical and mental health. It should not be used as a substitute for any treatment that has been prescribed or recommended by your doctor. The information within this book must not be construed as a medical, therapeutic, or psychological treatment, nor are any such claims made.

Every reasonable effort has been made to ensure that the material within this book is true, correct, complete, and appropriate at the time of writing. Nevertheless, the authors do not accept responsibility for any omission or error, or for any injury, damage, loss, or financial consequences arising from the use of this material. The authors, promoters, and publishers are not healthcare professionals, and expressly disclaim any responsibility for any adverse effects occurring as a result of the use of the suggestions or information herein. This material is offered as practical, current information available about disease and health management for your own education and enjoyment.

If you suspect you have a disease of any kind, it is imperative that you seek medical attention. It is also recommended that you consult with a qualified healthcare professional before beginning any diet or exercise program. By accepting this information, you agree to hold Keli Pitts, his associates, partners, and affiliates free of liability and damage, and you proceed on your own free will. You and you alone are solely responsible for the results that you produce. Do not continue unless you fully agree to these terms and conditions.

Register Your Book
& Get VIP Access
To Additional **FREE** bonuses:
(Journal, Bonus Content, etc.)
www.DoctorsOrdersBook.com

I dedicate this book to my mother and grandmother.
They were and still remain my first examples of femininity.
Here's and cheers to the most perfectly imperfect women in my life.
I love you very much "Mumzy" and Grandmama.

"Femininity is every woman's birthright, but some of us lose it along the way. Whether your femininity was not properly nurtured during your childhood or perhaps you gave it up after a series of failed romantic relationships, this book is for any woman who is desperately looking to find her way back."

-TFD

Oh! And I love you.

Contents

Acknowledgements 1
Author's Note 3
Introduction 7

PART ONE | WIPING THE SLATE CLEAN 13
CHAPTER 1: *It Will Take You!* 15
CHAPTER 2: *Forgive Others* 27
CHAPTER 3: *Forgive Yourself* 35
CHAPTER 4: *How Do You Feel About You?* 51

PART TWO | DEFINING FEMININITY 61
CHAPTER 5: *Damn! She's Feminine* 63

PART THREE | BECOMING MORE FEMININE 75
CHAPTER 6: *How Do I Become More Feminine?* 77
CHAPTER 7: *Become Worth Your Ask* 91
CHAPTER 8: *Get You Some Class* 101
CHAPTER 9: *Pay Attention to How You Carry Yourself* 115
CHAPTER 10: *Be Inviting and Warm* 125
CHAPTER 11: *Accountability* 131
CHAPTER 12: *Express Yourself* 141
CHAPTER 13: *Choose to See the Positive* 149
CHAPTER 14: *Keep A Grateful Spirit* 157
CHAPTER 15: *Resist the Urge to Gossip* 167
CHAPTER 16: *Take Pride in Your Appearance* 175
CHAPTER 17: *Grab A Hold of Your Finances. Claim Your Joy!* 185
CHAPTER 18: *Find Yourself in Feminine Company* 193
CHAPTER 19: *Get Excited About Men!* 203
CHAPTER 20: *Only Take Men Seriously Who Are Willing to Court You* 213

Final Thoughts 221

ACKNOWLEDGEMENTS

First and foremost I would like to thank my mother for giving me life. Momma, you always tell me stories of my birth and how from the moment you looked at me, you knew that I was special; that I was going to do something very big in this world. It means so much to me to know that I am your miracle baby. There's no way I would have made it without your patience, bravery, grace, and determination. Father, if this book ever finds its way into your hands please know that I pray for you often. In spite of where our relationship is today you are a part of my story, good and bad, and even though there was a lot of pain I fully understand why every little event in my life had to happen the way it did. I have no hate in my heart towards you or anyone else. I've got big work to do so I could not afford to remain on a path of brokenness. I hope that like myself, one day you'll find true joy and healing. You deserve that.

Thank you to my family! Wow! There are many wonderful adventures that stand out to me and you've been there for quite a few of them. Thank you for teaching me to place importance on people and relationships above all else. Thank you for instilling values in me such as honesty and charity. Thank you for always encouraging me to see the goodness of our God and his capabilities. As a child whenever I'd complain, grandfather and grandmother you were both always there to kick me in my backside (not literally hahaha) and say "now, you know the lord has been too good to you so you need to quit all that complaining". You were and are still right about that, my beloved grands, and I love you tenderly. How incredibly fortunate am I that you are both still here to see this book come to fruition. I hope that you are reading my words with the biggest smiles on your faces.

To my sister. You were born so kind, extremely beautiful and mild, and while you too have experienced a great deal of pain in your life, I pray that through my work you'll find yourself on a path of understanding and clarity. I love you; Jess and I wish you all the best!

Thank you to my friends, mentors, and my feminine community. You all inspire me and allow me to inspire you in return every single day. You've embraced me on my journey and my work would not be as possible without you! They say the day you find out what your purpose is, your life takes on a whole new meaning and while I agree, what would any purpose-driven human be without those who give them the space, trust, and authority to walk their path? Thank you so much for trusting me with your hearts. With your lives. With your femininity. I can promise you that if you keep on believing in me as *your* femininity doctor, your best days are ahead.

AUTHOR'S NOTE

First and foremost, from my heart to yours. Yes, I understand that probably would have been more appropriately placed at the end of this note, but the love I have for any woman who takes in this guide is what I have been waiting my entire life to express- and now here we are. You and I, getting ready to help you either reclaim your femininity or connect to it for the first time.

Secondly, I need you to know how thrilled I am that you have decided to embark on this journey. Woman. Beautiful feminine woman. Your life will be forever changed. I know where you have been, I know where you are now, and I know exactly where you have the potential to be. Do you trust me? Good.

Rest assured that I am qualified to guide you on the topic of femininity. Being raised by a narcissist took me away from myself at a very young age. Fortunately, though, when I was eighteen, I realized that I was severely damaged on the inside. That I was different from who I was as a child and without a doubt heading down a very dangerous path. I knew that I had to do something about this. To get back to a place where I was filled with joy. Back to a place where anyone who encountered me could tell that I loved life, truly from within. I am thirty years young today, and my twelve-year journey to healing not only revealed to me all of the parts of myself that were broken, but also that I was woefully disconnected from my nature. My femininity. How did this happen? Well. Several ways, but I believe that I should save that for another time. I will say though, that being deprived of true love, emotional support, and the teaching of self-awareness from the two people who brought me here was at the center of my pain. Naturally then, before I healed of course, I took my idea of what I thought love was along with my low self-image into the world; and I found myself in a cycle of even more rejection, fear, and mistrust in not only my romantic relationships, but also my friendships with other people.

The journey to healing was long, and at times it seemed never-ending. There were moments when I hated who I saw in the mirror. I was extremely uncomfortable and a stranger to myself as so much of the old me was leaving and a new person was taking form. I would repeat mistakes I thought I had overcome and there were times when I was frustrated to no end. Now, I understand that every up and down that I experienced was just a natural part of the healing process. I am thrilled that you have decided to embark on this journey, but I must confess that you too will feel lonely and frustrated at times as you're on the path to becoming your best and highest feminine self. BUT! Don't you dare give up and don't you dare

DOCTOR'S ORDERS

give in because there is so much goodness waiting to welcome you with open arms if you just keep swimming (you've seen the movie "Finding Nemo" haven't you?). Know that I am here for you and that all of the knowledge I have filled these pages with is yours forever. I love you so much and I'll see you on the other side.

INTRODUCTION

I believe it's pretty safe to say that I have been writing this book my whole life. No, I am not claiming that during fifth grade biology I was brainstorming on the title or what the table of contents would read (chuckles). When I look back over my entire existence though, I can honestly say that everything that's happened was designed to bring me to a place where I'm equipped to guide women to true happiness and healing. I have always been open with my community about my upbringing. What it was like being raised in a narcissistic environment, what that did to me at a young age, and just how long and hard I had to fight to get back to myself. Thirteen years of healing to be exact.

I remember being such a happy little girl. I was always so bubbly and filled up with fire and the wildest of dreams, but during my teenage year's things changed- specifically when I was entering high school. I guess you could say that this is when I started to feel my most independent. Naturally I wanted to express who I was becoming and what I believed in and while this was all too natural, it felt like my father saw my growth as some sort of betrayal; and our relationship turned a dark corner because of it. I no longer wanted the same things that he wanted and I wasn't afraid to speak passionately about it. I no longer agreed with him for the sake of keeping the peace in our home- as my mother taught me to do. My own heart and voice were too important to me and I knew that finding myself didn't make me a traitor in spite of what my father tried to convince me of.

A woman's father is supposed to be her first true love. It is his duty to protect her and be a sound demonstration as to what healthy relationships look like, but it's truly a tough burden to bare when you're under the leadership of a parent who lives with so much pain inside of themselves. So much pain that every single day, they find a way to make you share in that pain with them. Having to fight for peace day in and day out for so much of my life not only broke me, but it also hardened me; and even though I had no concept of femininity in my younger days, knowing what I know now has helped me understand how easy it is for a woman to lose her feminine energy and subconsciously trade up for masculinity when she is not properly nurtured.

I want every woman and girl to know that in spite of what has taken place in their lives, femininity is their birthright. It does not matter what has happened or what will happen for that matter, every woman is born with an innate connection to her femininity; and with a good foundation, proper training and direction she can find her way back to it. Some women have to work a little harder than others to reclaim their femininity and there is no guaranteed timeline for doing so. The journey to becoming a truly happy, healed, desirable, and wildly successful woman looks really unique for every individual as each person has been presented with a different set of circumstances. How long the journey to reclaiming one's femininity may be is not important so I encourage every woman to internalize this. What matters most is that she has made a brave decision by looking at her situation and deciding that she needs to get routed in the right direction. What's more impressive than the length of time it might take for a woman to get on the right path is her desire to become completely healthy. When a healthy being is the focus, the results are lasting which should be the goal for any woman who wishes to reclaim her femininity *for good*.

There is a ton of reflection and accountability that is getting ready to take place and you will be challenged with asking yourself some really tough questions. Breathe deep and know that it's okay because I am here with you. Know that *your* femininity doctor is here with you. I hope that you'll also find comfort in the fact that I've written this book in a way that makes it easy for any reader to follow along as this piece is divided into three main parts with its focus being on three main principles.

First, you'll discover exactly what it means to "wipe the slate clean" via forgiveness of yourself and others and then some inner reflection. That's right, potentially for the first time in your life you're going to have to sit with yourself and figure out exactly how *you* feel about you. This part is really personal as you can't rely on anyone else's opinion of yourself.

This time it's just you. I thought it would be useful to get you into the habit of self-reflecting by the way, and not just for the sake of getting through this book, but also for the sake of getting through life. Know that everything I am asking of you, I am asking because I have done these things myself; and it's because of these exact measures that I am able to enjoy being a light, free, sexy, vibrant, and desired feminine woman today.

Once you have hit the reset button, you'll move on to part two where you'll learn what femininity is- and I even help you discover a bit about masculinity too. Gosh, we love men, don't we? Ok! Ok! Hopeless girly rant over. Truly though, so many women are struggling with their femininity because well they don't even understand what it is. No one has ever sat them down to discuss what it means to be a woman *or* womanly. Additionally, they've never truly given much thought to the other side of the equation. The "ying" to femininity's "yang"- masculinity. It's no wonder then why many women spend their days as if they're dancing along to "blurred lines" by Robin Thicke because well, that's how they see femininity and masculinity. One big blurred line and they have no idea which side of the line they actually belong on. Get excited about part two because it is here to save you- literally!

The final section of this book, which is where you will spend most of your time is part three. I am thrilled that you'll be learning all about applying your femininity and making it work for you. Look out for the chapters where I discuss getting some class, being mindful of how you carry yourself, and finding yourself in feminine company. I had a ton of fun writing this book, but those chapters were extra an extra treat for me because I got to put a light and cheeky spin on some topics that are pretty critical, yet far too overlooked for by modern women today. I've also included some bonus 'notes' pages at the end of every chapter so that you can journal right here inside of the book instead of going elsewhere to keep track of your inner most feminine thoughts and feelings. I rock huh?! I'm only kidding. Enough of me joking around. You have waited on this very vital and life-changing information long enough so go ahead and turn the pages and get ready to walk towards the best days of your life! And hey! Don't forget to breathe. You *know* you've got this.

PART ONE

Wiping the Slate Clean

CHAPTER 1

It Will Take You!

I am more than overjoyed that you have decided somehow someway that there's a disconnect between you and your feminine nature. This is good as the first step to getting routed in the right direction is total honesty with yourself. So, before we embark on this journey together, take a moment and give yourself some credit for that. Are you ready? Let's do this.

Just about anyone who I have encountered has agreed that when they think of a feminine woman, or a woman who is truly operating in her element, they think of someone who possesses traits such as nurturing, soft, domestic, and warm. Other descriptive words have stood out to me of course, but for the most part these terms tend to be widely used when describing a woman's nature. In fact, when a woman confesses to me that she feels out of touch with her femininity, she usually considers herself to be the exact opposite of these things.

Before we dive in, you need to know something. You are a product of your experiences. Perhaps the women who were most influential in your upbringing, such as your mother and grandmother, were not the most feminine, so you never had consistently intimate examples of what this looked like. Perhaps you've found yourself in a cycle of romantic relationships where you were misled or taken advantage of so now you are having difficulties with being vulnerable or trusting others. Could you be someone who has always done every little thing on her own and as a result you became overly independent or developed what I call "fighter" syndrome, which is a response that causes a person to either consciously or subconsciously reject love and support from others? While being self-sufficient is a great achievement, never allowing anyone the opportunity to show up for you doesn't quite communicate that you believe you're deserving of adoration, servitude and love; which might be the reason you're struggling to attract these things into your life. If this sounds like you, rest-assured that you are not alone. I need you to know it and *internalize* it too. Women all across the globe are fighting something, even those who are *consistently* striving to be their best selves, daily. There will always be forces that we can't control. All you can do is remain committed to your ascension via honesty, personal accountability and love. If you can do this you'll remain on the right track, even and *especially* when it feels like you are not.

While what you are a product of may not necessarily be your fault, the healing from past traumas and the correction of toxic behaviors *is* your responsibility. I need you to believe me when I say that you can *and* will become the feminine woman of your dreams, but it will take YOU! From this day onward, you'll have to decide that you are willing to do whatever it takes to turn your ship around. Be mindful though, that ships are really lengthy on average- much like this journey that you are embarking on. Since this is the case, you need to be okay with the fact that it's going to take some time to completely turn yourself around. Ever witness a cruise ship attempt to head in the opposite direction? It's a bit of a slow process at first, and the captain and crew members may even find themselves a little impatient on the journey at times. Eventually though, the ship makes a complete 180 and gets going in the right direction; and just like the cruise ship so will you. Your journey to connecting with, or reclaiming your femininity will not be an overnight event. This is a process that you will have to dedicate yourself to and it will command a change in your overall attitude. There will be very little room for negativity, pessimism and excuses so fall out of love with those habits right now. Either you want this for yourself or you don't- and it really is that cut and dry.

This is all on you now

There can be no more blaming others! Those men from your past relationships who hurt you, for example, are no longer relevant; and if you're being honest with yourself there were some pretty critical signs and gut feelings that you ignored. The majority of my female audience confesses to me that one of the reasons they feel disconnected from their femininity is because they intentionally abandoned it as a defense mechanism with hopes of better shielding themselves from men who have bad intentions. I understand why this may feel like a good idea, but if you're going to move on and reclaim your femininity, you MUST believe in what I am saying as if your life depends on it- because it does! Your future, true happiness, and joy all rest in your hands so now more than ever it is important to look ahead instead of being tied down by your past. And isn't that good news? Doesn't it feel great to know that your destiny is *completely* up to you? Doesn't it excite you to know that there's nobody who can stand in the way of you having the life that you believe you deserve?

Mom could have had more talks with you about the importance of being soft or learning how to strut around in high heels, but you are becoming your *own* woman now. It's time to move on and let go of any and all resentment that you are harboring towards her too. If you hold on to the pain because you believe she failed you in some way, you're only going to make *some* progress only to find yourself right back where you started. You'll do this because by keeping yourself attached to the idea that your mother let you down, you're not clearing your emotional pathway for something new and better to take place. You cannot run a race and expect to actually win it with one foot in front of you and the other one behind you. Both feet must always be in forward motion. Blaming mom, dad, or whoever for that matter will only keep you stuck. Even if you do the work, you'll allow yourself to fall back on your disappointing past when it's convenient or say when this journey gets a little too tough. You will say things like "my mom never this" or "mom never taught me that" and you might do it without realizing that you are. To avoid this, decide *right* now that your past no longer owns you. Decide right now that whatever happened, happened and you cannot change any part of it! Your happiness is your responsibility now. All of it. So no more of the "this is just how I was raised" or "well this is just who I am" type of talk. Yes! That *was* how you were raised and that is who you *were* in the past- and the past could mean before you read the previous sentence. It doesn't matter though. The only thing that matters now is that you dedicate yourself to looking forward if you're going to master this journey to reclaiming your femininity *for good*.

Understand that you cannot go at this alone. You will need the love and support of those who are closest to you so make every effort to pull them into what you are doing. People don't just automatically know you are newly intentional about making some changes in your life and that's okay. Everyone has their own thing going on so when you need support, it's up to you to say so. There are a lot of habits that you're going to be working on doing away with and who you spend most of your time with you become the most like. So pull your loved ones in. For instance, you and your friends may have this habit of picking on women who are super girly and dainty. You are working on becoming your best feminine self now. Speaking ill of others and passing judgment on them is solely a reflection of what you believe you lack within yourself. Also, it's mean-spirited to judge another woman based on what you think you know and if you're being honest with yourself, you are only doing it because you wish you had the courage to embody more of what you see in her. Great news by the way. You do! You can absolutely tap into that same hyper-feminine energy that you secretly admire about another woman. That's right! You too can get to a place where you actually enjoy being more sensual, warm, sexy, and soft. However, these things won't be done successfully as you and your friends are tearing down other women. The next time you are with the group and this behavior starts up, let them know that you are working on being more positive and supportive of other women; and that actually, you admire a woman's confidence to boldly own her femininity. Encourage the conversation in a different direction and don't feel bad about it. Sure, they may wonder where this "new attitude" is coming from at first. Your friends may even think that you are not as fun to be with anymore or that you are "changing". You *are* changing so that's good! Hopefully, if you stick to your guns and refuse to partake in any mean girl activities, they will get the point and mature in this area themselves. If they do, it's a win-win because now you all get to reclaim your femininity together. If they don't that's okay too, but just know that you'll probably find yourself wanting to spend less time with them. Naturally. If you take this process seriously, you'll see that the people who don't support your commitment to growth will become less attractive to you- or at least less of a priority. No longer feeling aligned with people who you were once close to is normal by the way. It's so natural in fact, that I would be misleading you by not telling you to expect it. The old you is shedding and a newer version is taking form. Be more than okay with these changes! Just remember that your femininity doctor is going no place anytime soon. You will always have my support and you can't lose with that.

NOTES

NOTES

NOTES

NOTES

CHAPTER 2

Forgive Others

What I am about to say is serious so I need you to regard it as such. Are you ready for this? There is absolutely NO way that you can become a truly gentle, loving, vulnerable, nurturing, and feminine woman if you have *any* sort of unforgiveness in your heart towards others. Reread that as many times as you need to in order for it to truly penetrate because you can't afford for this not to sink in. You're being incredibly unrealistic if you actually believe that you are going to take this journey to reclaiming your femininity, and be successful at it, while at the same time being casual about forgiveness. I know that you can probably come up with ten-thousand reasons why the people in your life, both past and present, don't deserve to be forgiven for this thing or that thing. Trust me! I understand exactly where you are, but you're playing a dangerous game by choosing not to forgive them.

Ever heard of the saying forgiveness is for you, not others? Well, I don't think that anything could be truer; and I can tell you firsthand how unforgiveness is the thief of true peace and freedom. For example, I would *say* that I'd forgiven someone, but daily I'd still be fixated on painful events that took place with them. In most cases, the people who I was struggling to forgive were no longer in my life and had not been for a long time. While it was the mature thing to "say" that I was a forgiving person, I realized there were some people who hurt me too deeply for me to actually want to see them happy. By the way, if this sounds like you please know that you aren't a facetious person just because you're having a difficult time wishing someone well who hurt you. You are human and they caused you pain so honor that. I'm not saying that forgiving those individuals who let me down was easy, but I am saying that it was essential to my freedom and peace of mind and it's essential to yours too.

Before I decided to truly forgive everyone who had ever wronged me I found myself confused as to how I'd done so much healing, yet I still wasn't happy through and through. I thought about everything that I'd overcome and for a little while, I couldn't figure out what was left for me to do. I thought that I was on the right track when it came to forgiveness until it dawned on me one day to search my heart again. God spoke to me and said that ultimately, I had not forgiven everyone *completely*, and that harboring even just a tiny bit of anger towards anyone was going to keep me shackled to pain. In fact, it wasn't until I finally made the decision to live in total forgiveness that my life's purpose was revealed to me. Boy did that do it! If I wasn't sold on living a life of forgiveness before, gaining a better understanding of what I'm here to do with my life definitely sealed the deal; and now I am going to hopefully sell you on it too. So, hear me clearly on this one. Refusing to cleanse your heart of any ill is keeping you from so much more than you may realize. If you want to experience real freedom, start severing ties with unforgiveness that you're carrying for anyone and I do mean *anyone*.

As much as you may want to see a person feel the anger and confusion that they caused you, I am advising you to work very hard to fill your spirit with love, peace, and optimism instead. There are going to be times where you'll be tempted to go to a place of rage or frustration when you think about a person who let you down, used your heart to elevate their own ego, or just flat out took you for granted but don't! What has happened cannot be undone so there's no point in allowing it to reclaim your emotions. More importantly, your experiences happened *for* you not *to* you and the purpose of these life occurrences was to provide you with clarity on who you're actually meant to be. Keeping this in mind, there is no need to feel upset over your experiences- even the seemingly bad ones.

Forgive everyone! If you're allowing someone to remain in your life after they hurt you in some way, you're going to have to decide to completely move forward with a clean slate and trust them again. If you can't do that you should reconsider the relationship altogether. It's misleading to the other person(s) involved when you say that you're giving them another chance, but you don't actually trust them. If you just can't seem to get over what has happened while you're in contact with them, then be honest about it and wish them well.

If a person who hurt you is no longer in your life, then it is *especially* important to release yourself from them. Thinking about ways that they deserve to fail or hurt just as you did won't do you any good. It will only make you feel more pain overtime and keep you in a cycle of confusion and mistrust. Please take my word here. Whatever you must do to live in total forgiveness, do it and do it now.

NOTES

NOTES

NOTES

NOTES

CHAPTER 3

Forgive Yourself

Earlier I mentioned that you cannot truly become your best and highest feminine self if you do not forgive others and I'm getting ready to repeat something, which I'll do throughout this text when absolutely necessary. Ready? Here it goes. There is also absolutely NO way that you can become a truly gentle, loving, vulnerable, nurturing, and feminine woman if you carry *any* sort of unforgiveness in your heart towards yourself. I can recall an incident a couple of years ago as I was taking my morning shower when I screamed to the top of my lungs because as much as I thought I'd healed; I was still holding on to some residual pain. Truthfully, I had forgiven so many people, but there was one person I was forgetting about-myself. There I was. In my shower hunched over and very afraid. I couldn't believe that failing to forgive myself brought me to a place where the pain was so bad that it was literally trying to force it's way outside of my body. That moment changed my life forever. I knew that I needed to let whatever I was holding against myself go for good if I intended to be truly and permanently happy. Later in this chapter I'm going to revisit the topic of physical pain as it relates to forgiveness, but for now let's move on.

Forgiving yourself can be challenging most of the time because you can't figure out why you allowed yourself to be put through some of the things that you did. While it is healthy to reflect on the events of your past so that you do not fall into the habit of repeating poor choices, being overly hard on yourself to the point where you're struggling to forgive is dangerous *and* counter-productive. If you do not learn to extend this type of grace to yourself, you will make the road much harder and longer than it has to be. My journey to healing was thirteen years and I am one-hundred percent positive that time could have been cut in half had I truly understood what forgiveness entailed, why it's so vital, and who it cripples when not taken seriously enough.

Ultimately, our lives are about being taught things- and I believe that these things are designed to serve as lessons, and then tests. Once we pass these tests, we can graduate to the next phase of our lives and eventually, if we keep on going that is, we reach mastery level. Reaching mastery level does not mean that we are perfect, but we *are* more confident in who we are, why we're here, we walk more boldly on our individual paths, and we *rarely* make the same mistakes twice.

DOCTOR'S ORDERS

When you look at life like this, you'll actually start to feel a sense of peace. You will come to terms with the fact that you're here to excel, but it doesn't mean that you'll go through life unscathed. In fact, it's the scathing that makes you wiser and more gracious. You're not a fool nor are you are worthless because of your experiences. Whatever happened was designed for your betterment and it's a part of your journey to mastery. Breathe and tell yourself that it *happened*. Do you hear me? Whatever it is that's keeping you so disappointed in yourself has already occurred. You cannot go back and change any part of it. All you can do is sharpen your instincts and take any red flags into more consideration next time. Plus your best days are ahead so no more beating yourself up over the years that did not see you at your best. Forgive yourself and get excited about what's next.

I hope that you understand by now why living a life void of forgiveness is crippling and being in denial about your ability or inability to do so is only hurting *you*. Holding on to pain and anger can not only cause spiritual and emotional issues, but refusing to, or being slow to forgive may result in physical pain as well. Six summers ago, I visited with a round of physicians because I kept experiencing soreness in my muscles, constant headaches, shortness of breath, and stomach knots. Each doctor that would see me all came back with the same report, which was that my vitals checked out and I was absolutely fine. I knew something was wrong though. I could literally *feel* it. On my final doctor's visit the physician told me, just like all of the others, that she and her team could not find anything. She did pose a question to me though. One that I had never heard before. She asked me if I would consider seeing a psychotherapist. By the look on my face, I could tell she knew that I was dumbfounded by that question- and I was. For at least a second anyway. First, although I deduced based on the title that a psychotherapist had something to do with the mind, I wasn't sure what a psychotherapist actually did. Second, I didn't understand why in the world this physician was asking me if I had been to a therapist like that when the symptoms, I reported were physical. She explained to me that I was showing no signs of being sick or in poor health at all, and that possibly the real trouble was mental which might be causing me to *believe* that the pain was physical even though it was not. She recommended a psychotherapist to me and I left. As much as I was blind-sided by this news, what was going on with me made sense for the first time. I actually felt a sense of relief. Then, the relief turned into a bit of a sad "ah ha".

After more reflecting, it was clear to me that all of the doctor's I had seen were right. My illness, or problem, was not physical. My issue was rooted in my mind and in my heart. Thinking back on it, this might have been where I actually began to realize that all those sayings about forgiveness were much more than words pieced together, but that the act of doing so ought to be taken seriously. More seriously than I believe most people seem to understand. More seriously than I understood at the time. Here I was after several thousands of dollars spent on medical bills and so much time consumed, and all I really needed to do was *forgive*. Truly forgive. Since that day, I can honestly say that I've worked towards living in total forgiveness. Understanding what it looks like and dedicating myself to the practice until every single person in my life was forgiven.

First and foremost, mastering forgiveness will take work, but if you surrender to the process you'll feel much better about your life; and you'll attract better into it. Better relationships, people, opportunities you name it. Learning to forgive is tough and there will be some setbacks as you're working towards mastery, but whenever you are struggling to forgive repeat this to yourself: I am not okay with what happened. I do not like what happened, but I REFUSE to let it own me forever. Yes. I said "own" because holding on to resentment and/or anger means that you are bound and not truly free. Decide right now that there was a lesson in even the most unfortunate situations and that you're actually better off because you are more aligned with who and what is actually meant for you. You have no idea how adopting this attitude alone will set you free. Understanding that most people who come into our lives are just passing through to teach us something we need to know in order to go to the next level, but they aren't meant to stay with us long term. If you understand that most things are not meant to "be", you'll forgive a lot easier and a lot faster. Why? Because you'll realize that it makes no sense to dwell over someone who was just "passing through". So, commit to believing that although you are not *okay* with the disappointment or the pain, every situation has served a much greater cause; and because you get to be a better you as a result, you are no longer going to allow your past own you.

Remember this too! It is important to give yourself grace on this journey to total forgiveness. Sure, being hurt comes with rejection, fear, and paranoia and those are no small things. Even when you want to put your best foot forward, there always seems to be something from your past that shows up to remind you of the risks that come with letting go and trusting again. I have been there so know that I am advising you from a place of experience. It is natural to want to truly move on, but have some sort of fear showing up to haunt you. Fight every urge to give into this fear because well... it's just fear- and *fear* is only as real as we allow it to be. Seriously! When I was determined to forgive and be at total peace, I'd imagine myself as a boxer. I'd make a serious face and mentally start punching at negative thoughts and feelings that tried to make me believe I'd never be happy because of my past. Sounds silly, but it worked too! YOU are in charge so do whatever it takes to fight for your healing even if you have to picture yourself doing just that- fighting. Also, be patient with yourself in these moments. Breathe deep, and remind yourself that you are doing everything you can to be victorious over the doubts that have come to reclaim you. You might feel rage and sadness during those times when hurtful situations replay in your mind. This is especially natural when you are not fully over a particular person or event, but allow this negativity to pass because otherwise, you'll stay stuck in a low place longer than you have to.

When dealing with others it's important that you do your best to determine whether their actions are really aimed at hurting you or if you're just feeling uncertain about their intentions because you haven't fully healed from your past, thus causing unnecessary paranoia or mistrust. Right now, you're probably thinking to yourself "Of course I know when someone means well versus when I'm being overly cautious for no reason! This femininity doctor needs her own doctor." I'm not putting your judgment process on trial here in anyway, but what I am saying is that we don't always realize when we have left some things unchecked. I'll give you an example! I was recently catching up with one of my girlfriends, Kira, over some steak and wine when she told me that she was seeing a new guy. She seemed hesitant to fully let him in though because while he was saying and doing all the right things, her history with other men made her feel as if he wasn't being genuine. When I asked Kira to explain, she made statements like "he doesn't let me pay for anything when we are together" and "when I offered to visit him in his hometown, he insisted that he should come to me". Now naturally, I thought to myself that she may just finally have a true gentleman on her hands because well ladies, those do still exist! I detected no true red flags, but she was seriously worried that he saw her as an incapable woman who couldn't pull her own weight. She was also convincing herself that he didn't want her to come to his hometown because he was hiding her from another woman. This guy was doing *all* the right things like calling and checking in with her throughout the day, showing true interest in her life, and flying to see her and date her properly. However, she was convinced that something was *off* because this adult man didn't want her spending her own money or going out of her way to see him.

I decided not to take her concerns lightly, especially since I could see that her issues were not about this new guy at all.

My friend had been in several relationships with men who subscribed to "toxic masculinity", or a set of behaviors and beliefs that causes some men to see women as second-status humans. Oh, by the way. I came up with that definition all on my own so if you go searching for the *actual* definition of toxic masculinity and it's not written like that verbatim, don't sell me out to the rest of the feminine community, okay?! Alright, great. Not only had Kira been unlucky in her love life, she wasn't sure if she could trust herself again- which also meant she hadn't completely forgiven herself. I could clearly see that my friend was struggling to overcome her fear of romance because well, there was no real supporting evidence that this new guy had ulterior motives. I played devil's advocate with hopes of helping her realize that she was just afraid of being in a situation that was finally going right because she had subconsciously conditioned herself to expect for things to go wrong. I asked her if it's possible that he was raised by a man who taught him traditional practices, which makes him value being a provider so he prefers to pay and demonstrate to her what it looks like when a man shows a woman whom he's interested in a good time? I asked her if it was possible that he is just a mature man who believes that traditionally, when a relationship is new a man comes to a woman so she isn't taken too far out her way? At least until she feels safe enough with him? I suggested that he didn't sound like the kind of guy who thought little of her and that he was actually doing something called "courting". I explained that she might simply be experiencing unnecessary paranoia because men in her past have treated her like she was incapable of doing certain things. For the sake of moving on, I'll just say that it was nice to see Kira connect the dots after that. She actually realized she was dealing with a good guy who was only doing things that truly *mature* men do. This was an important step for her because it made her see that she hadn't fully forgiven herself or acknowledged the insecurities caused by her past, which is why she always felt like she was in harm's way even if she wasn't. Today, many of you are in the exact same boat as Kira was. You believe that others mean to slight you on purpose when really there's just more healing that needs to be done in those areas that are making you feel afraid. I am spending so much time on this because what I'd hate to see any woman continue to do is push good people away for no real reasons. So, while you're working towards living in total forgiveness, don't forget to stop and assess what is really going on in your own heart. Pay close attention to what you are feeling and do not neglect to be honest with yourself *before* making judgements in your relationships.

    I am not promising you that there won't be people who'll let you down as you're on this journey. Of course, you'll cross paths with individuals who don't have the best intentions and you will be tested many times. Still, give yourself every opportunity to be open because there is so much good out there and if you believe that, you'll attract far more of the good than the bad into your life. Trust me on this. When I decided that there are good people in this world just like there are bad people, and that I wasn't going to stop loving with my whole heart because of a few bad apples, I saw more success in my relationships. I really adopted the mantra that not everyone means me harm. Most don't actually. If you believe that people come into your life just to hurt you, you'll only attract more ill-intentioned people because what you fixate on manifests; and attracting more negativity will make you even *more* guarded and mistrusting of others. This is dangerous because it keeps you in a vicious cycle of paranoia, confusion, and exhaustion. If you're going to be successful at reclaiming your joy and your *femininity*, you simply can't afford this.

It's time to wipe your slate clean so that you can finally run towards your femininity and achieve lasting results. Again though, this can't be done if you are harboring any pain or bitterness in your heart. Depending on where you're starting from, you might need a little help on this journey with managing your healing so please allow me to make a suggestion. Are you ready? Get yourself some therapy. I know, I know. Therapy is for crazies. Well then call yourself crazy, find that therapist, and book an appointment! Look. A lot has happened and there is nothing, and I do mean *nothing* wrong with confiding in someone who can help you lay it all out on the table. I cannot tell you how much my life changed when I befriended a therapist. I can personally say that my faith healed me for the most part, but some good ole girl on girl therapy helped a ton! Talking to a professional who was able to guide me on connecting some dots was truly critical. Remember when I said that you'll need to be willing to do whatever it takes. Well. Here's to *whatever*. You can start small. Do whatever is budget-friendly for *you*. Perhaps a couple of sessions a month is exactly what you need. Just remember that the goal is to make sure you're consistently working towards being well

DOCTOR'S ORDERS

within. This is the only way that you can stay on the path to reclaiming your femininity for good.

NOTES

NOTES

NOTES

NOTES

CHAPTER 4

How Do You Feel About You?

Now that you're lighter and you understand the importance of wiping your slate completely clean, you can start focusing on how *you* actually feel about you! Not what other people have told you to believe about your person, good or bad, but what *you* believe. This, in my opinion, is where it gets exciting. Now you're probably wondering how this is exciting for someone who may not think too highly of themselves. Well, I'll tell you. The goal right now is to be realistic about where you are on your journey while giving yourself grace for everything that you've overcome. You might be a bit of a baby on this road to reclaiming your femininity, but rest-assured that some serious maturity is getting ready to take place- If you commit yourself to the process. My guess is you will since you've gotten this far. So, listen, even if you don't see yourself as someone who is completely gorgeous, lovable, and worth her weight in gold right now, start believing that you'll arrive at that place because this journey is just as much mental as it is emotional and physical. It doesn't matter where you are right now because your truth is your own! It's so special and personal to you, and THAT is exciting.

Now again. How do you feel about you? Ask yourself this question and be one-thousand percent honest. No one is around. It's just you and...you! Take some slow and deep breaths and ask yourself "how do *I* really feel about *me*?" Write these feelings down. Trust me. Write what's inside of you because I can personally admit that there is something about seeing your inner feelings laid out in front of you on paper that makes things more real for you. This will encourage you to actually face your reality which is exactly what must take place if you want to be free for *good*. Not only that. Even if you don't feel the most positive about yourself right now, when you're further along in this process you'll have something intimate to refer back to; and I can guarantee you that you'll feel a true sense of pride when you are quite literally looking at where you started in comparison to how far you've come and where you have the potential to go.

Now that you've gotten some things down- and trust me, new discoveries will be added to your list as you go along, tell yourself that in spite of what your reality is right now nothing on that list is going to stop you from doing what you need to do to become your most feminine, confident, nurturing, warm, adored and highly pursued self. Nothing and no one. The only force that can stop you is you. Understood? It's important that you get this now! There will be some speed bumps on this path and you will feel like giving in at times. You'll feel silly, misunderstood (even by those who love you), and a slew of other emotions. I have been there, but I am telling you that making it to the other side is worth it. Making it over here where you feel light, feminine, sensual, and excited about your life again is worth it. I promise you. Just keep breathing and know that I am here for you. My words are here for you. I love you very much. Yes? Ok!

I cannot see your list, but along with my personal experiences, I was inspired to create this body of work by a large community of women who have confessed to me that essentially, they don't *feel* feminine. That they don't know how to *be* feminine; and the narrative that seems most consistent at the core is this lack of connection to their actual nature. I just smiled because if you are like any of those women, we are getting ready to change all of that. *For good*!

Let's consider our nature for just one moment here. What comes to your mind when you think about a feminine woman? If you are having trouble coming up with something, it might help to recall some feminine women whom you have observed over the course of your life. These women do not have to be personally acquainted with you at all. They can be individuals who you have noticed in passing at the office or your church. It can be a woman who you watched a man stare at uncontrollably when you were out to dinner one evening or maybe this woman is someone who you know personally.

Women often tell me about that one woman in their group of friends who always seems to attract the very best of everything- and without even trying. That their friend just has *something* they don't believe they have for themselves. Friend or stranger, what did you or do you notice when you observe these feminine women? Take a moment and think about this. In fact, write those observations down on the opposite side of the sheet where you wrote how you feel about yourself. If you've run out of room, go on to a new page.

Now. I can't see this list either, but I am willing to bet a large amount of money that a few descriptive words are written down. Words like happy, fun-loving and loving, approachable, sweet, warm, bubbly, beautiful, well-dressed, sexy, open, and doesn't take herself *too* seriously. I am also willing to bet that I'd see words like honest, supportive, aware of what she deserves, confident, poised, graceful, and gentle. I could go on for days, but essentially what I think we can all agree on is that when we observe these women, we can tell that they like, love, enjoy, and take pride in being, that's right...*feminine*.

You're probably wondering what in the *heck* any of this has to do with femininity and how in the world it helps you. You might even be telling yourself that's just how *those* women are, that you don't have to be like them, or that you don't need to change who you are. Listen you can absolutely close this book and throw it in your existing pile of "bs", but that would mean that when you're facing something a little uncomfortable, you might be the type who gets dramatic and maybe just a tad defensive too. Imagine that I am there with you right now. This is where I smile and say "look at me. Am I right?" Ok. Now give me your hand because you and I are *not* enemies. We are on the exact same team, and while I am not here to change you perse; we have to get honest about what's just not working. Are you willing to do that? Good.

Now is a good time to address that you're probably thinking some of the traits I mentioned are not exclusively applicable to femininity. You might be saying to yourself that men can be happy, sexy, open and gentle too, for example. You're right! The point of my little exercise was to get you to think- and I know that I have. Like it or not though, it can't be denied that *feminine* women tend to possess certain characteristics which contribute to an overall womanly "essence"; and it is this beautiful essence that makes them undeniably magnetic, desired, an extreme joy to be around, and attractive to high quality people- especially high-quality men. I am not saying these feminine women are perfect or better than you, but what they've figured out is that the more they relax into their nature, the better positioned they are to receive *more* of what they want and *less* of what they don't want.

NOTES

NOTES

NOTES

NOTES

PART TWO

Defining Femininity

CHAPTER 5

Damn! She's Feminine

You are right! She certainly is feminine. And I'll tell you why you *feel* this way when you encounter a feminine woman. While her pencil skirts are beautiful and the way her hips dance when she walks is quite alluring, the most powerful weapon in her possession is understanding. An understanding of her nature- that is. Not only has she grabbed a hold of this understanding, but she actually enjoys what she knows, and what other women like her know too! Feminine women have figured out that an understanding of one's nature is the answer to many questions; and that the closer you are to your nature the more successful you will be. So, what is this nature I am speaking of?

Let's examine history for a moment. I have traced the sexes all the way back as far as the original man and woman, and from what I have observed, the nature of both sexes has not changed very much. I know what you are thinking! Today's men and women are *nothing* like they use to be. Men use to believe in headship and providing for the home, and women use to actually appear to enjoy being the caretakers of the children as well as submissive to their spouses. Well, this is actually still the case everywhere in our modern world. I am a frequent traveler who encounters all sorts of people so I see these things all of the time. There are still men who take pride in being the protector and the provider. Just like there are still women who love the idea of caring for the family, do not mind allowing her worthy and responsible man to lead; and these same women might just be CEO's now too since today's economy has made more space for gender equality in the workplace.

These things more so address "roles" that each sex is naturally aligned with *because* of their God-assigned natures though, but I still felt the need to address them just in case there was any thought that nature and roles were the same thing. They are not. Domestic, nurturing, gentle, soft, caring, alluring and kind are all words that can been used to define a woman's nature. These are all ways in which a woman's basic make up is described. Being in total understanding of your nature is where I believe every woman needs to begin. It is possible that no one has actually ever taken the time to truly dive into this with you on a deeper level, or perhaps so much has happened to take you away from your nature that you have simply forgotten what it means and why it's so important. It makes sense then why so many women just don't feel or know how to *be* feminine. Existing in your female body is not enough. You must actually understand your nature and then learn to operate in it at all times.

When a woman has decided that she likes, no LOVES being a woman, and above anything else, she becomes seriously unstoppable. Why? Because she is operating in her *natural element*. Show me one person who goes against their nature, yet claims to be truly successful and I will show you a liar. They do not exist. No matter how they appear on the surface, when a person is living in the unnatural for any reason, they feel a void within. I've witnessed this one-thousand times over- and I use to be one of these people. I always had a "womanly" appearance, but I lacked true inner joy during the years when my low self-worth caused me to court men or be overly- independent, for example. No. It was not until I decided to route myself in the right direction and stop fighting against what I later came to understand as my *nature* that I began to tap into real happiness. Myself and other feminine women have figured out that the woman was created to *be* a certain way- which for the most part is the complete opposite from man! We understand that just by relaxing into our femininity and fully operating in the natural we are elevated; and if you want to feel more of a connection to your divine feminine, you are going to have to learn to flow with nature instead of against it too.

You are not a man. I need you to read that sentence as many times as you have to for it to actually stick. YOU are NOT a *man* which is good news! Now in no way am I bashing men! I love them and everything about them, but like myself, other really feminine women understand that we are not "set up" like nor designed to be...men- and we are just fine with that. In fact, feminine women enjoy the fruits of their femininity *more* because they honor the separate yet *equal* importance of both sexes. I say this to women all of the time who reach out to me confessing that they are struggling with connecting to their womanhood, yet simultaneously refuse to give up their desire to "wear the pants", the need to prove they are just as tough as men, or their eagerness to compete with them. You just aren't a man. Trying to be like them, take on masculine traits or do the things that they do will only *confuse* you, and overtime you will become exhausted trying to be something that innately, you are not.

Feminine women do not try to *be* men. They may try to understand them, but they aren't actually looking to give up their femininity in exchange for masculinity- and why would they want to? They can't and shouldn't! Unfortunately, though, there are those who actually believe that being a woman means that you were dealt a lesser hand or that it makes you second class somehow. I meet women who see very little value in being gentle, nurturing, domestic, or anything that remotely reminds them of their femininity. They actually think that being too vulnerable or loving makes them appear immature, for example. Women like this have decided instead that they should air on the side of being more bullish, aggressive, overly logical and void of emotion. They believe that they'll be taken more seriously if they deny their femininity to become more masculine. Truly! These types view being "too feminine" as a sign of weakness and there are even some who shame other women for operating in their feminine nature too much- citing that they're limited or opening themselves up to be taken advantage of by appearing a certain way. While it may look like women who dismiss the importance of femininity or feminine characteristics are more stable on the outside, what you aren't seeing is the challenges they typically have connecting with themselves and others. They especially struggle emotionally because they have decided to turn that part of themselves off. They may not be outwardly vocal about their exhaustion with being overly independent, but they are. They may not say that they long for the support of others, especially the kind of cushion that comes with being in healthy romantic relationships, but they do. How do I know? Because these are the types of private admissions that I receive to my email *daily*. Masculine women, or women who are disconnected from their femininity are starting to realize that they bought into something that has not and can *never* work for them. In fact, most of them secretly envy feminine women. They desperately want to reconnect to their own femininity and start to see the same success and happiness that feminine women have because they've decided to embrace their feminine nature instead of throwing it away. I say, "reconnect to", by the way, because I believe that all women are born with an innate connection to their femininity.

It's pretty safe to say that you're serious about making some pretty necessary changes in your life if you are still reading this guide; and if I have not said it enough, I am beyond thrilled that you have decided to take this journey. It's going to be so worth it for you! From this day forward though, I will need for you to start loving and accepting the fact that you are a WOMAN! And that a man is a man- and that who you are and what you do is just as important. If you are going to fully relax into your femininity and start having some damn fun with it, you need to unfollow these lies that tell women we've been dealt the short-end of the stick. You know the ones that say we're oppressed because we don't get to *do* the things that men do or that there are double standards that work to keep us down? Yeah. Those! Truthfully speaking, women *don't* get to do all of the things that men get to do (and vice versa) and there are double standards that favor both sides. For example, men claim that our society does not embrace the idea that they can be as "expressive" with their feelings as women which can cause an on-set of emotional traumas for them. On other hand, women believe that when they are more sexually free with their bodies, they are overly criticized even though men get a pass for taking down as many women as they can. Obviously, there are far too many double standards to name so I won't be doing that here in this book. The point I am trying to make is that in order to really enjoy your femininity, you need to stop worrying about or comparing it to masculinity- at least in a negative sense; and you have to stop being upset with men because you believe that "the patriarchy" seeks to limit you. There will always be men who subscribe to toxic male behaviors just like there will always be women who see men as nothing more than financial foot stools. Pointing fingers across the aisle won't do you any good because there is blame to be had on both sides. Take it from me when I say that you'll only stunt your progress on this journey to reclaiming your femininity if you don't respect masculinity.

DOCTOR'S ORDERS

Remember that your goal here is to become a happy, healed, desirable, and wildly successful feminine woman so do all that you can to keep the focus on that.

Think about how INCREDIBLE it is to be a *woman*. Mmmmm. Let that sink in. You are a woah!man. A brilliant, out of this world, alluring, captivating, sexy, playful, charming, warm, talented and gifted woman. Close your eyes right now and tell yourself that there's nothing that you can't achieve and there's nothing that's too good for you. Believe it and receive it! God made you so unique and there are things that you were graced to do that a man simply cannot do. There are lovely energies and perspectives that you bring to the table that only a woman can so start living like you are the answer because you are. Start celebrating your femininity and falling so in love with the possibilities because the world needs that. The world will never not need femininity. The more that we return to loving all that we are, we will be better off as a collective. There is nothing like the woman and from now on, you are done believing that you are better off being anything else.

NOTES

NOTES

NOTES

NOTES

PART THREE

Becoming More Feminine

CHAPTER 6

How Do I Become More Feminine?

Now that you understand what your God-given nature is, let's talk about how you can reclaim your femininity or connect to it for the first time. What we are about to do will change your *entire* attitude. Are you ready? Good! Start by realizing the importance of your most primary characteristics, which are to love and nurture. The woman is the carrier of life in her womb, for example. Life is created and brought forth because of the woman. Yes, men help (chuckles), but humanity has permission to continue on because of what can be done inside of the woman! If every woman decided that her legs were closed for business, the world would be in serious trouble, but back to my point. You were made to nurture just as a man was made to hunt and protect. In fact, because a woman exclusively supports the life of another human being inside of her, it's a widespread belief that protection and covering are her birthrights. Only a woman is capable of carrying precious cargo of this kind- human life of course. This is one of the reasons that women are said to be a bit more vulnerable than men. A certain level of vulnerability is required, after all, to sustain life inside of the body; especially if that life is going to be successfully realized to term. Without women, humanity stops. Because of this, a precious commodity such as the woman should be protected and adored by all means. Stop for a second and let that sink in. A precious commodity such as the woman should be protected and adored by *all* means. You were made for many reasons, but the ability to create life in and of itself is a huge, huge deal. If you can really see the value in that alone, you will start to feel a deeper connection to your femininity. You don't need to actually have children or even want any of your own to understand how special being capable of such a thing truly is. So again. You are a commodity. You are to be protected, respected (first by yourself), and adored. Now, in no way am I saying that men aren't important or that they should be treated like less than. I am simply encouraging you to operate with the understanding that the woman is very unique and that there is no substitute for who we are, what we have, and what we can do; and anytime there is no substitute for something, whatever that "something" is, it becomes especially invaluable.

While we are on the topic of becoming more feminine, you should resolve to only be in the company of energies and people who have the utmost respect for women. Today, we live in a culture that glories the degradation of women, our bodies, and our sexualities; and the consequences are extensive. TV, social, and music media are the most influential means of consumption because the average person does not go one single day without utilizing at least one of these mediums; and the message is consistent across all platforms. What message exactly? That the woman's value lies mostly in her body and her sex- and not in a positive way such as the reproductive capabilities that I mentioned earlier. I cannot turn on my TV or open up any one of my social media apps without seeing a woman being degraded in some way; and if you aren't careful about limiting how much of this content you consume, these demeaning perspectives about women will seep into your subconscious too. Believe me I know. I'd say that I'm a respectable woman, but there are times when certain songs come on the radio and I find myself really intrigued by the beat and high energy of the music. Sure I know better and I don't actually believe that a woman should pimp herself out to any guy who is flashing fancy jewelry and a lavish lifestyle in front of her, but music is influential and before I know it I'm swaying along to messages that are actually very diminishing.

In no way am I saying that women can't compartmentalize. What I am saying though is that words have real power and you can subscribe to something without knowing it if you consume whatever *it* is long enough. Enjoy yourself, but if I were you, I'd limit taking in disrespectful and devaluing content about women. Doing so starts off harmless, but before you know it being called "bitch" is not an insult, it becomes "cool" or normal; and dancing provocatively in front of a large crowd doesn't seem like such a big deal because you see it in videos. That is until you're categorized as the girl who men have fun with, but refuse to introduce to their mom. This happens a lot and women find themselves confused as to what the problem is or why they can't actually attract quality into their lives. They don't seem to understand that you become what you consume whether you know it or not. If you are always around disrespect, you will become disrespectful- even towards yourself. If you are always hearing about promiscuity and sexual looseness, you will become casual about giving away your body because you won't think that sex is a big deal. Of course, until you are having children out of wedlock with no prospects for marriage in sight.

    What you are surrounded by matters. The content that you hear and see. The people that you are around matters because these things shape who we become. It's really sad to see women agree with certain aspects of our culture that promote toxic images of femininity and fail to uplift them. Sadly, they realize later on in their lives that they bought into complete nonsense. Then they have to pick themselves up, retrain their minds and get routed in the right direction; and this is usually after they've had enough of being overlooked and taken far less seriously than those women who knew better than they did earlier on in their lives. Believe me, you will save yourself a ton of time and heartbreak if you don't go down this wild anything goes type of path. You will feel far more beautiful, valuable, adored and yes, *feminine* if you simply decide to keep a close eye on what you are inviting into your environment.

While we are on the subject of "environments", let's have the sex talk. Yes. The *sex* talk. More specifically, I want to address the well-known slogan "pussy is power". Why? Because it is so don't you dare just go giving your precious power away! Now I'm not saying that women do not enjoy sex *too* or that women have not gone out of their way to have their sexual needs met. Nope. I am not saying that at all, but where have you ever heard of a saying such as "penis is power"? You probably haven't! And there is a reason for that. What a woman has in between her thighs is not just the gateway to the creation of life, it is the warm and soft path to pleasure. Yes. Pleasure. Release. And comfort! I have dated plenty of men, observed them in their natural habitats, and I've had many conversations with girlfriends and guy friends. The attitudes that women have about sex with men do not compare to the attitudes that men have about sex with women. Not even close. While I can personally attest to being a woman who enjoys sex, I also need to form a connection to a man before I truly "go there" with him. I have never had a one-night stand, for example, and if I am unable to see myself in a committed relationship with a man, sex isn't even an option. On the other hand, just about every man who I have encountered believes that sex is more like causal fun for them especially if they're not in a committed relationship. One of my closest guy friends once told me that men will do anything, and I do mean *anything* for sex. That is why they lie, cheat, manipulate, go out of their way for it- you name it. This confession stunned and amused me, but it made sense. Essentially, he was saying that most men believe that they *need* sex to survive and to feel complete. He explained that it also helps them cope with the societal pressures that are placed on them such as having to be the bread winners, appear very tough and masculine all of the time or never feeling safe to express their emotions. Once I was dating a hard-working man who made millions for himself at a very young age, and as handsome and accomplished as he is, he once told me that he'd literally have sex with just about any woman. He could get the most stunning and beautiful female to be on his arm, but he seriously made such a statement. Naturally, I was turned off as I could not see myself in a seriously committed relationship with a man who would be with *any* woman, but after my emotions settled, I realized what he said wasn't breaking news at all. In fact, it made me recall several past exchanges with other men. He was just re-iterating what I had already heard countless times before which is that sex is really, really important across the male diaspora. No questions.

I want every woman reading this book to stop for a moment and ask yourself the following questions. Would I do *anything* for sex? Would I have sex with just any man? Is sex serious enough to me at all to the point where I cannot go without it for any period of time? Most of us, if we are being totally honest with ourselves are not willing to go out of our way to have a man penetrate us and we are not going to have sex with just any guy – at least I certainly hope not. We also know that historically, the act of sex has been more serious for women. Typically, our emotions become completely entangled with a man whom we have had sex with and so naturally, we want more out of the relationship. More could be an exclusive commitment, a marriage and family, or just more alone time and affection. However, we usually want more. I have been there and I have witnessed other women end up in similar situations as well.

Why am I saying all of this? What does sex have to do with reclaiming or connecting to one's femininity? Well, I mentioned earlier in this text that the woman has been exclusively chosen by God to carry and bring forth life, and this unique capability is one of the things that makes us a commodity. Well, the same goes for your sex. If the general attitude amongst men is that sex with *us* is VERY serious to *them*, that they need it, and will do quite a bit for it; I believe that we can safely assume that the very thing just beneath your waist is a commodity too. Now, in no way does this give any woman a pass to be manipulative nor should she place an extensive amount of her worth on her sex alone, but If you haven't figured out what I am saying by now, I'll just go ahead and make it plain for you. Your very femininity is significant. It, in and of it itself, is a commodity and it is necessary.

If you didn't' know, now you know. Your womanhood is *essential*. This should excite you and by now the wheels should be turning in your head. If they are, good! Otherwise, allow me to officially walk you over the line. You have something that men don't think they can live without (their words, not mine). Your womanhood is beautiful and of great value. You should treat it in as such and always be selective about who has access. Doesn't this make you feel good? Doesn't this make you see yourself differently? Doesn't knowing that your femininity is so highly sought after make you feel unstoppable? Giddy? Girlish? Happy? Adored? Curious? Yes. Curious! Doesn't knowing all of this make you think to yourself, hmm! Since my womanhood is so precious. Since my existence is in demand for various reasons, and I have full control over who has access to me, doesn't this increase my likelihood of getting what I want if I apply myself? If I hold myself to a certain standard and honor my femininity first? Doesn't this make it easier for me to just relax thus allowing the desires of my heart to flow in my direction with more ease? Are you starting to feel more connected to your feminine power? I certainly hope so.

While we're on the topic of feminine power, be sure to keep yours by staying away from people who don't make you feel loved. You know? Those people who do not respect your feelings or rarely make you feel seen. These people are the worst kind of people and one of the biggest threats to the feminine spirit because our spirit needs support and protection. You can understand your nature, watch what you consume, and be very selective with the men you go to bed with, but you'd still be missing an important piece of the puzzle if you are constantly choosing people who make you feel bad about yourself. Anyone who gaslights or denies your feelings, for example, is not truly in the relationship for you. This applies to friends, family members, and romantic partners. It doesn't matter. Limit your time with anyone who does not wish to see you happy. And if you can help it, just avoid them altogether.

DOCTOR'S ORDERS

You will endure unnecessary heartache if you make yourself available to thieves of joy. Remember that.

NOTES

NOTES

NOTES

NOTES

CHAPTER 7

Become Worth Your Ask

Before going any further, I want you to stop and give yourself some major points because you have made it this far into "Doctor's Orders". To know that you are changing and growing as you're reading my words means more than I can say. Thank you for wanting to understand more about your femininity and for realizing you needed to embark on this journey for yourself. How beautiful is it that you recognized there was a disconnect between you and your feminine nature thus you decided that just wouldn't do? I am so excited that your life is changing and if you'll have me, I can't wait to be a part of your very best days.

So, what does becoming worth your ask mean exactly? Well, it's simple. Make sure, as much as possible at least, that anything you ask of others you first are yourself. I am saying this because I do not hear this being told to women enough and it's so vital that we do not skip over this part. The last thing that you want to do is be in expectation of qualities and characteristics from others that you cannot give in return. It is unfair, distasteful, and unrealistic. Thinking that you are overly worthy while failing to work hard on your own heart only means that there is a strong disconnect between your perceived self-value and your actual worth. People treat you according to who you are, not according to how you believe they should.

You do not need to be perfect to be worthy of all that you ask- not even close. To attract quality though, you have to *be* quality or at least be working towards it. If you want relationships with people who are accountable for their actions, for example, then you should hold yourself to that same standard. If you feel respected and secure when others communicate with you, then communication should be one of the strongest weapons in your arsenal. If you value vulnerability because it helps you feel more connected to others, then you too must be willing to put yourself out there. Failing to hold yourself just as accountable for the things that you require from others only makes you look like a hypocrite. An entitled one. Nobody wants to feel as though there is a double standard when they are dealing with you, and it will especially be a turn off for anyone who values their own sanity. If you want to have successful relationships with others, you'll need to quite literally "practice what you preach" as much as you can. This high value behavior will be especially attractive to other high value people because it says that you are about equality in your relationships. Qualities like this are rare and it will help to set you apart, and when you are set apart, you're eligible for much higher things. As a result, your confidence will increase which makes it easier for you to reclaim your femininity for good.

So how can you actually ensure that you are a woman who is worth her ask? Well, there are many steps that you can take, but if I elaborated on every single one of them, we'd be on the topic all day. So for now, I'll just walk you through some basics. First, work at becoming principle-centered. When you are principle-focused, you make decisions based on what is objectively right. This might feel like more of a sacrifice than you care to make at times, but it will keep you on a straight path, a purpose-filled one, and this is something that other high value people will be able to detect in you. For example, a principle-centered woman is all about fairness and respect. She holds herself to these same standards and she keeps this in mind when dealings with others. A principle-centered woman will not be in a relationship of any kind with someone who is not respectful of her. Respect might range from expecting the people in her life to keep their promises to being honest and integral in tough situations simply because it is the right thing to do. Either way, it's a practice of quality feminine women to be about principles, and they don't make unnecessary excuses for anyone who is not principle-centered themselves.

Be about what you say you are about in all that you do! I know that you've heard that before, but you'd be surprised at how little people actually do it. So! If you want to *be* worth your ask, then you'll definitely need to implement behaviors that are in alignment with what you speak. This is important because it communicates to others that you have integrity, you quite literally mean what you say, and you hold yourself accountable to the same things that you hold others accountable to. Talk is nice, but actions are what get you the respect that you're after. By the way, it's so much easier to relax into your femininity when you feel truly respected. If your actions line up with your words it means that you're being truthful with others, but more importantly it means that you're being truthful with yourself. This can be seen and felt. Not only that, being about what you say you are about in word and in deed is such a high-quality characteristic that attracts even *more* quality into your life. So simply put, say what you mean and mean what you say.

Finally, do not forget to lead with love. This can be tough especially for anyone who's been through a lot or has had their kindness taken advantage of on a consistent basis. I have been there more than you know, but take it from me when I say that you should never stop leading with love. It doesn't matter what happens, dust yourself off and do your best to act with grace and kindness. This is freeing and it demonstrates courage. Why? Because not every woman honors her femininity by doing so even though it's in our nature to love first. I know what you're thinking! Doing things with or out of love has only *led you* to the slaughter house. Right? Or you are probably telling yourself that coming off as too nice opens you up to being taken advantage of. I am not saying that every single person who you interact with is going to see and appreciate your efforts. What I *am* saying is that leading with love will pay off for you gradually- and certainly really big over time.

DOCTOR'S ORDERS

Take it from me! I have always wanted to love first, but there was a period in my life where I became extremely hardened and mistrustful of just about everyone. This resulted in major consequences though. Not only did it make me all sorts of sour on the inside, but I also attracted other really unhappy people into my life. Which makes sense if we consider the laws of attraction. Whatever we are and whatever we believe results in what we attract. It doesn't matter what we say out of our mouths, who we are on the inside is proven by who and what shows up on the front doorsteps of our lives. Be wise. Use your beautiful feminine instincts, but take the high road and move in love so that you can secure your lasting happiness. Finally, attracting more love and support closer to you because it's who you have decided you are first will definitely aid you in becoming worth your ask and *reclaiming* your femininity for good.

NOTES

NOTES

NOTES

NOTES

CHAPTER 8

Get You Some Class!

I don't care how much the world changes. Class *has* never and *will* never go out of style. One of the sexiest things about a woman is the way that she presents herself and class is a huge part of this. I don't think that a woman's femininity can be denied when she prioritizes good manners, humility, and empathy for example, which are all true signs of class. We all know the difference in how we feel when we come into to contact with someone who is classy versus someone who is not. A person with class tends to hold the attention of the people who they encounter in a way that someone who lacks class cannot. A person with class has an easier time being liked by as well as being influential over others while a person who demonstrates very little class is not; and a person with class tends to get exactly what they want out of life which isn't on accident.

It is far better to be a woman who is classy and has classy habits than to be one who isn't and doesn't. Trust me. I constantly see women complain that they are overlooked or rarely taken seriously. When I actually observe these types of women though, whether it be through personal exchanges with them or by some other means, I notice that they have very little *class*. While not being taken seriously is an unfortunate thing, I'll tell you this: whatever energy you put out into the ecosystem is exactly what you'll get back in return. Nothing less and certainly nothing more. You cannot speak ill of others, for example, and expect that good and gracious things will be said about you. You can't look down on or judge others harshly, and actually expect for people to enjoy your company. And you *cannot* expect to take yet want others to give, give, give unto you. Life simply doesn't go this way. Please stop believing that you do not have to show any class or any kindness, gentility, and grace and then expect for favor to find you somehow. It's okay if you've never heard it put quite like this before. Now that you have, you should take this very seriously and adjust yourself accordingly.

Becoming a quality woman does not just happen. Either you were raised to be a woman of high value or you learned to do so through your own personal experiences. It doesn't really matter *how* you get there, it only matters that you do. Why? Because women who are of high value and seek to show class in all that they do attract energies, relationships, and opportunities that women who are not of high value and class cannot.

DOCTOR'S ORDERS

When you attract exactly what you want it gives you a certain confidence. A feminine confidence that can make you a magnet for exciting possibilities. However, when you're made to settle for things because you haven't done the work to *become* the kind of woman who is eligible for what you desire, it takes *away* from your feminine confidence which can make you unpleasant and bitter. As a result, you find yourself in a cycle of more toxicity. More anger. More pessimism. You get the point! It does not have to be this way for you, but you must do the work because doing the hard work on yourself is what elevates you and sets you apart from other women.

Stay away from drama at all costs as it does disrupt your spirit and takes you off of your path. This is serious and I see women get caught up in this lifestyle all of the time- almost as if turmoil is an innate part of femininity. Truly. Steer clear of drama as much as you can because it is high class repellent and it will make you appear shallow. Ever meet a woman, or maybe you have someone in your life who always seems to attract *drama*? Literally wherever they go, drama follows? Or perhaps, nothing is ever going right in their lives and no one can seem to figure out why? Take some time to think about how you feel when you are around this person. Have you ever felt overwhelmed, on edge, or maybe even a bit sad when you are with them? Have you ever felt like your mood goes from high to low the minute they come around? That's energy! *That* is your spirit telling you that this person is probably doing way more taking away than adding in life. *That* is your spirit telling you that this person is connected to other elements that may not necessarily align with your values; and by association, you may find yourself caught up in their web of narcissism and confusion over time.

People who are attracted to drama have not figured out the true meaning of happiness. Heck! They *are* unhappiness, and they are only drawn to chaos because it makes them feel a little less insecure about what they lack within themselves. I once had a friend named, Rina and she absolutely *loved* drama! In fact, the very first time that we went out together for cocktails, an argument between a couple broke out at a booth not too far from us. She noticed the exchange between the two rather quickly and immediately turned her attention away from our conversation to dial in on the couple. It was truly the most bizarre thing as I had never seen someone go out of their way all just to witness *drama*. I looked into her eyes as she watched the pair do their back and forth and she was excited. Our relationship was pretty new, but it was the most thrilled I had seen her since we met. I ignored it at the time, but I remember feeling off when I arrived home later that night. I couldn't understand why she was so aroused at the sight of two people having such an unfortunate exchange. Don't get me wrong, it would've been one thing to notice what was going on, have a little giggle over it and then keep on moving, but she had enjoyed the back and forth a little *too* much.

Needless to say, my friendship with Rina was pretty short-lived as it turned out what happened that night we were out for cocktails was not a one-time thing. On more than a few occasions, she would go out of her way to see a fight or listen in on an argument and to me, being around her just got plain ole weird sometimes. I knew very early on that she and I weren't exactly cut from the same cloth, but I really wanted to like her so I gave our relationship a chance. The more time that I spent with her though, my gut feelings proved to be right on! She had strong ties to drama which revealed themselves to me via her relationships with other people! Just about every time we would get together, she was either venting about how someone upset her or she'd be gossiping about something totally awful in general; and before I knew it, I started relishing her chaos as well. All of a sudden, I was interested in other people's business far more than I'd normally be. There was even a time or two when I caught myself saying things I had no business saying. I felt cheap quite frankly. Like I was speaking things into my life that I knew weren't right for me. I stopped feeling like a high-status woman when I was around Rina and I knew that if I didn't want to adopt her pessimistic attitude about life, I needed to distance myself from her totally- so I did.

Do your very best to avoid being self-centered as this, in my opinion at least, is one of the least classy things that a woman can be. It doesn't matter how great you look or how successful you are, an egocentric person is a total turn off! Why? Because self-centered people always come with risks and getting involved with them usually means that the other person will be putting far more into the relationship than they get back out of it. Self-centered people are very good at getting what they need from others, whether it be emotional support, financial support etc., but it's usually at the other party's expense. They put their desires first without really thinking about how they affect other people, and after a ton of time loss and valuable resources spent, they drain almost anyone who cares about them.

You do not want to be known for taking or using people to prompt yourself up. Without a doubt, this will lessen your prestige, turn quality people off of you, and as a result you will have a challenging time connecting to your femininity; and it'll be this way because you rarely experiencing meaningful, long-lasting relationships which causes a void in your life. You'll always second guess yourself and you'll think that you aren't lovable because people don't seem to stick around for very long. People don't detach themselves from self-centered people because they aren't likeable perse, but they do so because a relationship with them feels more parasitic than equally beneficial. If you are struggling in this area start correcting it now! Not sure if you're self-centered? Ask a few people in your life what they think and do NOT lash out at them if they tell you something that you may not want to hear. It's childish and manipulative when you ask someone to tell you the truth, and then you attack them because the truth made you uncomfortable.

Work on being as selfless as possible every single day. You can start small and then go big. Do more kind deeds without expecting anything in return. Truly listen to your friends and loved ones, for example, when they open up about matters that are important to them. Make every effort to see where and how you can improve in every relationship. Really see the value in being genuine and thoughtful. Now, you may see a slow turn-around and you might even continue to have interesting luck in your relationships even though you are working hard to implement these changes. That's okay! Remember. You are doing this for you. You are growing into a highly feminine, mature woman for *yourself*, so you'll need to fall in love with playing the long game because your growth will not always be met with instant gratification. When you're feeling a little frustrated, just remind yourself that you are dedicated to being your best regardless of what happens; and because you are so committed to this journey you *will* find yourself living a happier and more fulfilling life overall.

Be mindful of the words that you speak! Be mindful of the words that you speak. We live in a culture that glorifies negative speech- and it's gotten all too bad. Words. Are. Not. Just. Words. They are extremely powerful and they seep into the subconscious. Our music and media are two very strategic tools and presently, they are making us think that this isn't the case. That everything is happy go lucky and *nothing* is a big deal. We are being seduced into believing that the words we say and the things we do don't have important consequences, but really this is just desensitizing us to very serious issues. Words are not just words. They DO matter, and what you speak does have the power to alter your reality. Don't believe me? Why do you think that certain words are used in particular spaces? When you go to the spa, the hostess greets you with jargon that makes you feel warm. Welcomed. Relaxed. Right? You might hear phrases such as "how can we serve you today?" or would you like some "*warm* tea and maybe a *soft* towel?" It is set up this way because you are in an place where the goal is to get you to come undone and forget about your worries. Oppositely, when you are in an action-oriented environment such as a nightclub or a rock-climbing arena, you might hear words that get you pumped; and it's because people who are in charge of marketing experiences to others understand that words *are* influential and they have the power to create new realities (both good and not so good). The very same thing applies to you.

Speaking of words, let's talk about a couple that I especially encourage my feminine community to stay away from! They are "bitch" and "hoe". I do not care what society tells you. You do not look "cool" when you call yourself or anyone else, a bitch or a hoe. These words, and their associates, are a huge part of the cultural problem that we are facing today. When you use terms like "bitch", "bad bitch", "that bitch", "this hoe" and "that hoe", what you are essentially telling the worlds is that you have limited respect for yourself. Believe what you wish, but no woman who is mature, classy, socially and personally aware speaks this way. They just don't! They understand that words are an extension of what a person feels on the inside. In spite of what modern feminine culture promotes, bitch and hoe are not terms of endearment. If you want to be a *truly* feminine woman, you will need to start being more mindful of your speech. I'm not saying that you can't have fun or that you should take yourself too seriously. We all joke around with girlfriends or colleagues, for example. Still, I'm encouraging you to practice using more tasteful language because you don't want to struggle with doing so when you need to the most.

Can you imagine attending a gala for charity or a BBQ filled with your potential husband's friends and family and calling someone really important in the room a sexy bitch? Sure, you might mean it as a compliment, but I guarantee you that your score has dropped and when your name comes up at a later date, and it most certainly will, people might say something along the lines of, "I thought that she was lovely until she opened up her mouth". Sound familiar? Good. Because it happens. No one should have to explain your shortcomings and the world doesn't have to pardon your ignorance. Taking more care of your speech is a responsibility that rests solely with you. If you actually believe that being sweet, pretty, or a "good person" are enough to get you by, you are wrong. Completely wrong. Far too often, I see women make excuses for their poor habits because they think that being well-intentioned and easy on the eyes is enough. This is actually what I call "toxic femininity", which is the belief that for some reason, or special set of reasons, the rules that everyone else has to abide by do not apply to you. If you subscribe to this way of thinking, stop doing so immediately! If you want to become the kind of woman who is respected, adored, and highly sought after, which will only increase your feminine confidence, you have to be fully accountable for yourself. Being mindful of the words that you speak, and when and how to use them, plays a huge part in this.

NOTES

NOTES

NOTES

NOTES

CHAPTER 9

Pay Attention to How You Carry Yourself

Don't just pay attention to how you carry yourself in public. Do so in private too! If you are always mindful of how you carry yourself, you won't have to remember to be at your best when you are in the company of others. You will naturally just *be* your best because it's who you have decided you are no matter where you go or what challenges may come your way. Watching your posture, being mindful of your language, and making sure that you always appear clean and properly dressed for all occasions are just a few things to consider when thinking about how you carry yourself, but these are good places to start. When you carry yourself well, people treat you well. They take a second look at you and regarded you with more care and respect. Why? Because carrying yourself well is a sign that *you* respect *yourself* so naturally others will follow suit.

Let's discuss posture for a moment here. I recall being a young girl and anytime I would "slouch", my mother and grandmother would immediately tell me to "sit up" or correct my position. Naturally, I didn't see the importance of what they were saying at the time. I thought that they were just nagging me for no reason and that if slouching made me comfortable then I should be allowed to do just that. As I got older though, my mother and grandmother made more sense to me. It is important to implement good posture because it's one of the ways you tell the world how you feel about yourself. Poor posture communicates that you don't feel powerful or worthy, maybe even that you don't fully respect yourself. It might also signal to your audience, whether it be your peers, superiors or your lover that you don't appreciate their presence or that you aren't fully engaged during your time with them - and you definitely don't want that.

Good posture is just important and that certainly goes for women which is why I feel it's necessary to address in this guide! When you show up in the world, you want others to receive you like someone who is to be taken seriously- because you are. But first, you need to believe that yourself. Poor posture doesn't quite send the message that you. are. worth. it. Whatever *it* is, you're *daggon* worth it- and when you actually operate in worthiness, others will take notice and treat you accordingly. As a result, you will feel sure that you are in fact on the right path! As you continue down this path, seeing the way that the world opens up to you will increase your confidence. Remember! The more vibrant and confident you feel, the easier you'll find it to relax into your femininity! Make sense? Good!

One more thing. Watch the way that you walk. Yes! You read that correctly. For the sake of stressing how important this is, I'm going to repeat myself. Pay attention to the way that you walk. The next time you get up to walk around, do so with intention. Actually, notice how you move. Do your shoulders and neck hang low? Do you look towards the ground? Do you drag your feet? Here's the honest truth. Are you ready?! How a woman walks is very telling as it is one way that she non-verbally communicates what's happening on the inside of her. Women who take pride in being feminine, confident, and beautiful tend to express these things in many ways, especially when they set their bodies in motion. Women who do *not* feel so great about themselves tend to drag their feet along, hang their heads low or are just sloppy with their movement in general. I remember being out to lunch one day when I found myself sort of people watching. I like to do that a lot actually. Anyway, as I am sitting at my booth journaling and waiting on my food, a woman glides in and quite literally commands the room! Everyone stopped what they were doing to notice this 5'7 feminine goddess. I am sure that part of it was because she was so beautifully dressed, but the way that she walked was alluring and unmistakable! All I remember thinking was "wow. Just wow". She always put one foot in front of the other. Her legs were very direct and guided. Her shoulders were back. She was upright and her breast were perked up instead of weighed down. It was definitely safe to say that she was happy and successful at *something*. Her walk pretty much told everyone in her path that she was not afraid to own her womanhood and that she expected to be treated like the feminine, radiant being that she is.

I kept observing this woman. All of the waiters went out of their way to pass by her table to make sure she had everything she needed. The manager stopped by to host conversation several times and when she got up to go to the washroom, every single person made room for her; and not once did I notice her open her own doors! It was really refreshing to see another woman receive this treatment because so many women claim that they struggle to own the room in social settings or that people don't go out of their way for them. If you are a woman who feels unseen or irrelevant, I want to tell you this: people see you how you see *yourself*. If you carry yourself like someone who isn't sexy, feminine, or important then that's the energy the world will give you right back. I don't make the rules, but I do understand them very well! I am an attractive and confident woman who is optimistic and expects to attract quality which is why I walk like it! I don't want anything that is not of great value to show up in my life so I carry myself like I expect the best because I do! Much like this woman, people and especially men- handsome men, go out of their way to open doors for me. I get asked if I need anything just about anywhere I go. Complete strangers approach me to make conversation and I always attract good energy. This is not solely because I am physically attractive. I am one-hundred percent positive that it's because I tell the world just what I expect by the way that I present myself. I want you to know that you can experience this treatment too! I want every single woman reading this guide to feel just as good about themselves as myself and the woman who strutted into the restaurant that day feel each and every time, we are reminded of how refreshing owning our femininity is. If you remain diligent about doing all that it takes to walk in *your* divine feminine, the world will open up for you too.

NOTES

NOTES

NOTES

NOTES

CHAPTER 10

Be Inviting and Warm

Some of you might think that acting snooty or unapproachable makes you look hard to get and for some women, this might even work. For the most part though, you'll give off an energy that says you don't actually want to be approached. This may keep unwanted company away, but it will also keep very *wanted* company away. No one, and I do mean no one of quality who values their own sanity is going to willingly approach someone who gives off a less than friendly vibe- and why would they? You are your best advertisement so remember that. Would you further inquire about an ad if it read "Caution. I am mean, cynical, and unhappy"? Now don't go making excuses or looking for exceptions here. The answer is no! No. No. and No. The only people who situate themselves around others who are unhappy, are they themselves *unhappy*.

So, remember that! I know that you have been through a lot. Maybe even nothing but unfortunate things. You are not alone. Today though, you have decided to become an incredible feminine woman so it's time to move on in optimism and good faith. It is time to radiate warmth, joy and excitement if you want to live a life of true wellness and there is no better time than now to make some necessary changes.

One way to be warmer and more inviting is by smiling more. Even if you have to force it a little at first, it will start to come to you naturally over time. I smile and I speak to just about everyone who I cross paths with and I cannot tell you what a difference it makes in my world! For the most part, I get nothing but positive feedback and it's because I give off an energy that is inviting. Yes, I sometimes attract people who I may not fancy all that much, but in those cases I politely decline their advances. Listen, people want to be around, with, and do for those who make them feel good. Sincerely smiling tends to send the message that engaging with you will bring about good things and we *all* want to find ourselves in the company of goodness. So remember! Even if it takes you out of your comfort zone at first, do your very best to be warm and inviting.

NOTES

NOTES

NOTES

NOTES

CHAPTER 11

Accountability

Oh, woman. This one is so important as it will undoubtedly make a world of a difference in who and what you attract into your life. Now, I did warn you that I would be redundant at times, didn't I? Well, here is one of those times. If you really want to reclaim your femininity, and reclaim it for good, you will need to become an accountable woman. That's right! A-C-C-O-U-N-T-A-B-LE. For yourself, your life, everything. Listen, I understand that things happen and sometimes these things are beyond your control, but you only get one life. That's right. YOU only get one life and you would be much better off in it if you learned that you are not a victim. This is not to take away from people who are actually victims of misfortunate such as domestic affairs, for example. That is *true* victimhood. What I am saying is, when I started to understand that even though I could not control others but that I am in control of who I am and what I'm about, I saw my life change for the better. Little by little sure, but I could see clear improvements when I stopped believing that every little thing was happening *to* me instead of happening *for* me. I made it my business to look at every situation that I was a part of, both past and present, and instead of pointing the finger at the other person, I asked myself two things: what is/was the lesson in this for me and what could I have done differently? So, accountability for yourself, your life, and anyone who you allow in it is critically important.

While we are on the topic of accountability, I have a little secret for you! Becoming accountable communicates to others that not only do you have little interest in living life as a victim, but it says that you also value practicality, or at least to some extent. This is extremely attractive to other high-quality people and especially high-quality men (inserts wink)! A woman who is mature enough not to blame shift or make others responsible for her problems is admirable! And its sexy too. I've dated men who have expressed how they rarely get this from women and how refreshing it is to finally be with one who chooses not to resort to such dramatics. You will be elevated in the eyes of others when they see that you're a woman who respects herself enough to take complete responsibility for her life. Being elevated to a high-status woman is special and a confidence booster; and by now we know what happens when a woman feels confident in herself. Yup! You guessed right. It becomes *that* much easier for her to relax into her femininity.

DOCTOR'S ORDERS

Holding yourself accountable can feel like hard work at first, but you want to make it your business no matter what because it will keep you honest with yourself! When we are honest with ourselves, we are more aligned with who we truly are. Take it from me when I tell you to get clear on what it is that you want for your life today because if you don't, it'll be difficult to have any real success. If you don't become so sure on what you are holding yourself to, you'll float along and while that's cute for teenaged girls, it will make *you* look uncertain. If you want to become the kind of woman who is respected, trusted, desired, and so much more, take accountability for yourself and your life to heart. For example, if you want to date commitment-minded men and make an exceptional amount of money then make a plan, work it, and keep yourself accountable for that plan! You can even share your plan with an accountability partner who you trust and do not go give up on the plan when turbulence comes up -and trust me, it does come up. Truly though, accountability will make all the difference in whether you end up living an average life or one that most women only dream of. Today, I am extremely happy to be financially secure and living a life filled with purpose, but I can honestly say that I wouldn't be here had I not adopted an accountable mindset earlier on in my life.

I especially preach the importance of accountability because I know how much *more* happiness I experienced when I decided to be completely accountable for my attitude- starting with my attitude towards anger. For example, staying angry with anyone for a long period of time kept me living with one foot outside of joy; and a woman's inner joy is one of the things that makes her the most attractive! By taking control of my anger, it became easier to reject anything outside of myself that wanted to claim power over me. Know that if you commit to changing your attitude towards anger, you will experience freedom like you never have before. You may not realize it yet, but just like forgiveness, deciding to keep negative emotions in check is essential to becoming your most desirable, feminine self. Keeping yourself accountable for your anger will determine what this journey looks like for you.

Being as happy as possible was always the goal for me, and I found that not only can I attain it, but that I could keep it for good. How did I find lasting happiness exactly? Well self- control was a part of it- sure, but learning to hold the people in my life accountable proved to be just as important. Holding *yourself* to a certain standard is great. It really is and if you've mastered that part you should be proud, but you're only doing yourself half of the justice that you are owed if you let others come into your life and run a complete muck. Do not do this. There are rules, requirements, and regulations for just about everything in life, so why should you be any different? Far too often, women tell me stories about how they became so mistrustful of others and there's always a common theme: people who came into their lives to take advantage of them. When we get into the details of their relationships though, I find another commonality which is that they *all* failed to set boundaries and then hold these people accountable before things got out of hand.

Listen. I completely understand that it is in a woman's nature to believe the very best about others first, especially those who we cherish. Sometimes in the process of doing so, we can overlook the importance of consequences- and I'm saying "we" because every now and then I catch myself doing it too. We typically do this because we are afraid of something; and so instead of allowing ourselves to be absolutely clear on what we need from the people in our lives, and holding them accountable if they fall short, we silence ourselves to avoid confrontation. Hey, in no way am I judging you and I don't think that any woman who is struggling in this area is weak. Like I said! I've been there and on occasion, I go back there. However, doing this means that everybody wins except the for the intended winner- you! And since you have got a long life ahead of yourself hopefully, why be here to lose? Exactly! So, get confident in expressing yourself and know that being uncomfortable is a natural part of the process.

Hold any and every one accountable! If you find that a friend or a lover fails to keep their word about something, do not normalize this. It'll only make you resent them. If a coworker who you find yourself teamed up with often fails to meet important deadlines, report this to your superiors and ask to be reassigned to someone who shares the same work ethic as you. Do not fool yourself into thinking that you're "uncool" or "inflexible" because you refuse to accept unfair treatment. The only person who loses is you when you are complicit with less than favorable actions and if anyone expects you to be its because they themselves are low value. You are not *here* to be low in value so get clear on what you deserve and become extremely comfortable with holding others accountable. Remember, It's going to feel uncomfortable at first and slightly confrontational too, but over time you'll get much more confident at this; and it is this confidence that communicates to others that you know what you deserve. So! Never be afraid to hold others accountable. Just be sure to do it with diplomacy and grace and I guarantee that you will change what you attract. Then, watch your feminine confidence soar!

NOTES

NOTES

NOTES

NOTES

CHAPTER 12

Express Yourself

That's right! Learn to be okay with expressing your thoughts, needs, expectations, and everything in between. Far too often women write to me saying that they are horrified to express what it is that they are feeling. What it is that they *really* need. Usually, they are this way because either they were not taught to express themselves by their parents and teachers during their primitive years *or* they stopped doing so at some point in their lives out of fear of being labeled too combative, a nag, scorned or problematic. Listen! Take it from someone who was never really taught the importance of knowing that my voice mattered either-not until I reached a pivotal point in my womanhood at least. Silencing yourself does far more harm than it does good; and ultimately, you're saying that you're ok with putting the needs and interests of others over your own. I understand that considering others first comes so naturally for most women and while it can be a beautiful thing, it should never be done to your detriment. It also doesn't mean that you are not allowed to speak up about what is important to you. If you have been taught to fear expression, I am here to help you unlearn that right now.

Hesitating to express yourself doesn't mean that you stop wanting to be heard, and it doesn't mean that your needs simply go away. You are only creating unnecessary chaos for yourself because the more you feel unheard, the more resentful you will become. When you live with resentment, you don't trust others and eventually you stop trusting yourself. Have you ever heard of the saying that silence is compliance? Yes. That can apply to your relationship with yourself too! Ultimately by staying silent when it comes to things that you know you ought to express, you are agreeing to the treatment that you are receiving. If you aren't speaking up, what you are non-verbally communicating is that you're okay with what is happening to you. No truly. When you do not speak up for yourself, you are in agreement with whatever is displeasing you. So, speak up woman! There is a way to do it that will get you positive results especially when you are dealing with other healthy people. Not sure if you are dealing with these types? Expressing yourself will definitely expose who is genuinely in your life to add value versus who is around for their own gain. Either way, their honest intentions will be exposed. If they want to see you benefit from the relationship too, great! Give them the appropriate amount of time to make the adjustments which should lead to clear and positive changes. If you are made to feel like a burden for expressing yourself, then the relationship might not be worth investing in any further. No matter how you slice it, you know where you stand which in my humble opinion means you're much better off.

You are probably wondering how in the world you are supposed to go from being someone who speaks up for their themselves very little to someone who is a master at making their position crystal clear. Well, the truth is this transition will take a little time and that's okay. Learn to enjoy the process of reclaiming your femininity because as I mentioned at the beginning of this guide, you are *on* a journey. You will not master it overnight and why would you want to? Nothing that is rushed is permanent, and we want you to reclaim your femininity *for good*. So, here's how you get really great at expressing yourself. With respect and clarity. Yup! That's it. Think about what is important to you and exactly what it is that you need *before* making your claim. When you are clear on what you want and what you need, the likelihood of actually getting your way increases. Also, when you approach a situation with strategy and diplomacy, i.e. saving the drama, it is more likely that the other party will find favor with what you are saying. Why? Because when you are rational and respectful, the lower the chances are that they'll feel attacked. The exchange will merely resemble a conversation being had between two parties who first respect themselves, and then each other. With that in mind, what I am about to tell you is critical when you're dealing in relationships of any kind so please do your best to remember it if you actually want to get your way *and* keep the connection strong with the other party. Approaching any situation with unstable emotions, an accusatory tone (some call this blame speech), and/or unreasonable expectations will cause the person(s) to shut down, even if they appear to be engaged. It's possible that the other individual(s) may not have intended to do any harm and they probably had no idea you felt taken for granted. In other words, most of what takes place between people that leads to ill feelings usually stems from a misunderstanding; and so even when it's difficult, it really is best to just keep a cool head.

Approach the problems that arise in your relationships like negotiations because well isn't everything negotiable- including our problems? Simply explain to other party what you need and what you feel calmly and with respect, then give them an opportunity to do the same. If you don't see any real changes over time then you may not be in a situation where you are valued. If this is the case, then you will need to ask yourself if the relationship is the right fit for you. If at any point you decide that it isn't be prepared to move on.

NOTES

NOTES

NOTES

NOTES

CHAPTER 13

Choose to See the Positive

Or in other words, do everything that you can to keep an extremely positive outlook on life. Want to feel divinely connected to your femininity? Choose joy no matter what because in doing so you will feel lighter, happier, and yes! More feminine. Sure, there will be times when you are tested and being on the "up and up" is going to feel unrealistic. Give yourself grace in those moments, but do not resolve to stay in a negative space for too long! Trust me. The longer you do, the more challenging it is to recover positive feelings. Actively *choosing* to see the positive might be a new concept for you, but it really does work. You can take a situation and decide to see it negatively or positively, but rest assured whatever you *choose*, will make all the difference in your life.

Understand this too. You are always choosing. We all are. If you are currently living life like a victim or believing that you are not in control, I strongly encourage you to do away with this kind of thinking. Fast! Nothing positive flows from victimhood. Good or bad, you have a choice in how you go through life and how you respond to what takes place in it. I can personally attest to what *choosing* positivity has done for me. Once I understood the power of choice, I saw a shift within myself, and it was because I realized that I was more powerful than anyone had ever told me that I was. I learned that even if I am not necessarily responsible for what is happening, I could still choose how I react to it. For example, I may not be able to control the fact that another person can't see my worth, but I *can* choose to remain secure in my own value and then decide to be in the company of those who *do* see my worth. A person who believes that they are a victim might see the situation through a negative set of lenses. Instead of refusing to allow their value to be called into question, they might choose to become emotional or desperate for acceptance. Not only does this waste precious time that this individual cannot get back, going this route can be seriously damaging to their self-esteem. So! It is always wise to choose to see the positive and then allow that choice to open you up to better possibilities.

Choosing the upside typically yields positive results for you when others may not be having the same luck. Many times, I have been in situations with loved ones and had a totally different experience than the other person or group that I was with. I remember being out to dinner with a good friend of mine a few months ago and she insisted that our waiter was rude. When I asked her what she was making reference to, she mentioned things like he looked at her funny and that he didn't seem very excited to be taking care of us. She even went as far as accusing him of being a sexist. Naturally, I was a little blown away she concluded that our waiter was sexist because he was not the friendliest person in her opinion. Not only was the accusation heavy, but I personally did also not detect any sexist behavior from him. I decided to play devil's advocate when I suggested that maybe he was having a bad day and that his energy had nothing to do with her. Maybe he and his boss had a disagreement just before we walked in. Perhaps his attitude was not work related at all. He could've been behind on bills, struggling in school or a number of other things. Thankfully, she agreed that I had a good point and decided to let it go about halfway through our meal. I'm pretty sure that this made a difference in her experience because once she decided to drop her suspicions and just be friendly towards our server, the air around us got so much lighter! This was really great, but imagine how much more fun she would have had if she *chose* to be positive from the very start. She spent nearly forty-five minutes annoyed and who knows how much beauty she missed out on because of it. What if a handsome man noticed her when we sat down at our table, but decided not to approach because she appeared to be upset? What if someone who thought about coming over to pay her a compliment decided that she did not seem that attractive after all because her attitude overtook her looks?

There are many reasons why people do the things they do and you won't always understand what those reasons are, but it won't add any value to your life if you choose to be the kind of woman who assumes the negative first. Trust me. Being positive and encouraging others to do so is rare because most people assume the worst. It's good to be rare like this because it sets you a part in a way that is extremely attractive. Furthermore, being positive just encourages others to be closer to you and it'll make you feel so good that you are desired because you bring about a sense of peace. This is so important to note because there are going to be times on this journey to reclaiming your femininity when you aren't so sure if doing the hard work on yourself is paying off, but rest assured that it is so keep on going.

NOTES

NOTES

NOTES

NOTES

CHAPTER 14

Keep A Grateful Spirit

Here is where I may lose some of you, but I need to touch on this topic anyway. No one, and I do mean *no one* owes you anything. This might feel like a bit of a gut punch for you especially if you've gone your whole life with this idea that things should be given to you or that people should go out of their way for you all because you're a "woman". Yes, the woman is special. My position on this has not changed at all. I still believe that women are to be protected, and adored, but this does *not* mean you should approach life with a sense of entitlement all *because* you are a woman. Many of you may refer to this as "princess syndrome", which is a sickness that makes women and girls out of touch with reality. It's okay to believe that you are royalty especially if you're working extremely hard to become the best version of yourself. What's *not* okay is behaving distastefully or immaturely because you have a false sense of self-importance.

Keeping a grateful spirit is a sign of humility and worldliness. It shows others that while you know you are worthy of good things, as we all are, you appreciate and show gratitude for the goodness in your life regardless. While you play a part in attracting the good that happens to you, it is healthy when you recognize that something much higher than or outside of yourself contributes to this goodness; and since this is the case you should always be giving thanks.

Having an attitude of gratitude is responsible and it makes you a joy to be around. It will also make you a magnet for more positivity-whether that be positive people, energies, and opportunities while others may not be so fortunate because they are not as grateful as you are. I make it my business to be grateful for everything that I have. Even if I have a moment of weakness, I do my best to quickly reverse my attitude to gratefulness again. I do this because I know what a difference it makes in my day-to-day life. I can especially feel the difference in what I attract and how things play out for me in general when I take a grateful approach versus an ungrateful one. Attracting good things and living the life that I deserve because I choose gratefulness makes me feel joyful; and it's because of this joy that I have an easier time staying connected to my femininity.

Do not take the importance of gratitude for granted especially since you are looking to be more connected to *your* femininity. Women who live the lives that they desire all have things in common and gratefulness is at the top of the list. How can you become more grateful? There are several ways!

One of the most important ways that you can become more grateful is by resisting the urge to complain. Regardless if things are going great or just downright awful, do your best to keep the complaining to a minimum because it, whatever "it" is, could really be so much worse. I do my best every single day to grow a little more in this area. When I find myself complaining, I take a moment to ask myself what in the world I am actually complaining about? And usually, it's nothing. At least not in the grand scheme of things. So, the next time you pull up to the bank, for example, and the line is really long or you start thinking about the fact that you are not making the kind of money that you'd like to be making right now, resist the urge to complain. I get that life has its frustrations, but what would complaining do other than put you in a bad mood which usually makes you feel even worse about your situation? Instead of choosing to complain say to yourself that the only reason you are even at the bank is because you have money to either deposit or extract; and well if you truly want to make more money find a way to do that. Whether it be locating a twenty-five dollar course that teaches you how to trade stock options, picking up a retail job at Saks Fifth Avenue, or going to your superiors about a raise, challenge yourself to look for alternatives instead of complaining about your situation.

Get yourself a journal and write in it daily! I prefer to do this at the end of my day as I am reflecting on all that took place in it. I write down the good and the *not* so good. Doing so gives me the chance to see my reality laid out in front of me which makes it easier for me to do some good ole comparing and contrasting. I mostly write though because when I look back over my life and just how much things have changed, it's easy to remember how blessed I am. Journaling and reflecting remind me that I am on the right path, and who in the world would ever be ungrateful for being on the right path? Moral of the story? If you want to become more grateful yourself, invest in that journal and start keeping good records of your life. Being able to track all that has happened, how you grew from each situation, and what you did with that growth will definitely come in handy during those seasons when you need your own gentle reminders.

Commit to staying in the present! How often has a good time or positive energy been ruined because you allowed yourself to start worrying about yesterday or tomorrow? Yeeeaaaaah. Guilty huh? That's okay. Go on and plead the fifth if you have to. I can personally admit to living with this bad habit for so long until one day I realized that I was voluntarily sabotaging my own happiness. Upon noticing what I was doing I asked myself "aren't you tired of worrying all the time?". "Don't you just want to be happy?" and "why are you doing this to yourself anyway?". There have been periods in my life where several moments throughout the day, I would be having an amazing time and then I'd interrupt that good time by worrying about something I might have said yesterday or something I needed to do the next day. I was making myself so very sad and totally on purpose. I knew that this was not the way. I knew that I didn't want to look back on my life and never be able to recall a time when I was truly happy or at peace. So, I did what I needed to do to change that. I started to pray about this. A lot. Essentially, I knew that this was a battle of the mind and my faith teaches me that with prayer and dedication, even those battles can be won. And won it was. I'd say to any woman who wishes to live a life of gratitude that prayer, mediation, and honoring something outside of yourself can be life-changing. And I am not just saying that because it sounds super righteous. I am saying it because it's true and I am a living testimony.

Not everyone is spiritual or religious, which I totally respect. The goal is to get you on the path to happiness which is a major key to reclaiming your femininity *for good*! If you don't wish to pray or meditate, write down some positive affirmations and keep them close to you at all times. Like. Really close. Perhaps next to your bedside, near the steering wheel in your car (nothing that will block your view of the road of course), your purse, or maybe even your pocket. Make sure that these affirmations remind you to think of the good things that you have going on and *definitely* make sure they remind you of the consequences that come with not practicing gratitude. Three or four daily affirmations should do the trick. Commit them to memory and say them to yourself slowly as much as you can. Perhaps you could turn them into a catchy song and riddle them off extremely fast. Do whatever it takes to remain grateful though, and watch your life change for the better.

NOTES

NOTES

NOTES

NOTES

CHAPTER 15

Resist the Urge to Gossip

---⸺ঌ৫৫⸺---

Avoid getting mixed up in the habit of gossip as much as you can! I understand that this isn't always so easy to do as certain aspects of modern culture promote seeing people exposed, ridiculed, canceled and everything in between. Gossip is everywhere. If we are not consuming it on our tv screens, it's in the music that we listen to, and it even shows up in spaces that claim to promote sisterhood and female empowerment. There is always pressure to partake in this meaninglessness, but it doesn't mean that you should- and for several reasons. First and foremost, it's just plain old mean. I know it's easy to forget that there are real people on the receiving end of your ridicule, but there are. It's *especially* easy to forget this when life is going well for *you*! Sometimes, we live in rose land and we to tend surround ourselves with people who live there too; and while happiness and success are not crimes, you should always take into account that not everyone is doing as well as you are. Someone we know might be experiencing a shift in finances or issues within their marriage. While these things may be tempting to discuss with others, know that there are real people with real feelings involved. So please *don't* be one of those women who forgets this when the opportunity to speak on someone else presents itself.

It helps to show others grace. After all, hardship will find its way to you too at some point because no one goes through life completely free of adversity. Things will not always be just perfect and I know that you, like anyone else, would want others to show you a little common decency by not speaking on your business. You know that it would suck like hell to be at the center of someone else's conversation in a less than positive way, but as the old adage says: "what goes around, comes around". If I were you, I would keep this one pretty close to your heart. Now I am not saying that there's anything wrong with catching up with girlfriends and having some cocktails over a little girl talk. However, be sensitive to what gets said and be especially mindful of when you or someone else in the group might be going *too* far.

When it comes to friends, family, or anyone really my personal rule of thumb is that I do not repeat anything that would make someone feel ashamed or embarrassed. If I have to second-guess whether the other person would be okay with what I said should my words ever find their way back to them, then I *definitely* keep it to myself. Even if I am asked about a situation by a mutual friend for example, I keep my feedback both general and objective. I have been in many situations with a group of girlfriends and while we may all be privy to certain things about a loved one of ours, I will still only say so much, especially if this person has shared more information with me that they've kept from everyone else. You should never take it for granted when someone trusts you because trust really is hard to come by. If you are ever asked about a person or situation and you get a funny feeling on the inside, respectfully decline to answer because it's usually a sign that you have no business speaking on the issue at all. If the party inquiring gives you grief about your decision or even assures you that they won't repeat what you say, you can politely inform them that they'd get the same level of respect if someone asked *you* about *them*.

Staying away from gossip is one of the truest signs of maturity because it says you're secure enough in who you are that you don't need to partake in things that make people look bad. It also says that you have got more important things to focus on and that you are more invested in improving yourself. This is so refreshing and rare, and its especially attractive to the opposite sex. I hear men say all the time how sexy it is when they meet a woman who doesn't or rarely gossips because most women who they know do it so often. Men don't mind when you vent so don't go thinking that you can't let your hair down or be honest about what's on your mind, but be mindful of what you say. For example, a coworker can get annoying and maybe you don't have any allies at the office. Perhaps your cousin always needs you to give her advice, but she can never give you any in return. Telling him that your coworker doesn't play fair and it's frustrating you is quite different than calling him/her out of their name and wishing that they'd lose their job. Men understand that life happens, but do your best to keep your venting above board. Besides you don't want a man to start second-guessing how you talk about him when he's not around because of the awful things he hears you say about other people. The goal is to relax into your femininity by understanding the beautiful power in it, but you should never be the kind of woman who uses her femininity as an excuse to tear people down.

NOTES

NOTES

NOTES

NOTES

CHAPTER 16

Take Pride in Your Appearance

I could pretend that looks don't matter, but they do and if you want to attract the very best into your life then you better learn to take pride in your appearance. I know, I know. You're rolling your eyes and telling yourself that this guide is some shallow bs". Listen to me. You can slam this book closed and then go and tell the entire feminine community that it's trash, but I need you to ask yourself this first? Have I steered you wrong yet? If the answer is no, then keep reading. If yes, I still think that you should keep reading. You can convince yourself all day long that looks don't matter. That appearances *don't* matter. That physical fitness or having a great sense of style aren't really all that important. However, I am here to tell you that you've been woefully misinformed and that you MUST stop lying to yourself about this. Starting today, I want you to get serious about your outer appearance because it matters almost as much as what's on the inside of you.

So, first and foremost, get in the best physical shape as you possibly can. Not only does research show that people who maintain great physical health and wellness tend to be happier and more successful, I can personally attest to how much my life improved when I started eating for my blood type and working out four times a week, minimum. I was never physically unappealing perse, but I was not always at my best. I knew it and my body knew it as well. Adopting a lifestyle where I committed to *High Intensity Interval Training* workouts, drinking alkaline water with a PH of 8+, and eating lean proteins and veggies (with some sweets here and there) greatly improved my health and visual appearance; and can I let you in on a little something? I went from attracting playboys to men who were just as handsome and successful, but actually commitment-minded. The more I began to attract commitment-minded men, date them and be around their friends, I noticed that for the most part highly desirable men tend to choose more physically appealing women. And I am not just talking about *any* type of men. I'm talking about the kind of men that most women would be proud to be with. So if you are in the dating market and you are seriously looking, you will want to increase your chances of attracting the top of the litter. One of the best ways that you can do this, in addition to being mentally and emotionally healthy of course, is by taking pride in your health and physical fitness.

DOCTOR'S ORDERS

You and I are about to play a little game because well, I like those. Let's pretend that you are out to a cocktail parlor with friends when you notice that there are some pretty attractive men in the room as well as some who are not so easy on the eyes. Who are you more drawn to? C'mon, be honest. There's no one else inside of your head right now so the Mother Teresa thing is a wash ok?! By default, you know that you are far more intrigued by the guy who is dressed in a nicely fitted top and slacks, neatly groomed and carries himself with masculine sexual confidence. In no way are you shallow for not being as drawn to the guy whose outfit could use a little bit of tailor work, slouches, and doesn't seem to be as confident in why he came. Well, the same goes for women too. When a woman looks as though she takes care of her body, is beautifully put together in maybe a dress that tastefully flaunts her curves and a stunning pair of pumps, and walks into a room with feminine confidence, people take notice. Why? Because outer appearance is one of the ways that we communicate to the world what might be going on inside of ourselves. When a woman looks well, what she's saying without saying anything at all is that she recognizes her own value and that she knows she's too good to present herself any ole kind of way. Because showing up in the world just any kind of way might communicate that you do not care what you attract or how you come off. This approach may work for the pink-haired rebel types, but that's a different conversation. Since you are on the path to becoming your most desirable and successful feminine self, it is not wise to pretend that your appearance isn't important because it certainly is!

The next time you are out and about, take a little time to just "people watch". Try to spot a well-dressed woman and maybe one who is not put together quite as nice. Notice the difference in how they are treated, and if you are looking through an objective set of lenses, you'll *definitely* notice the difference. I am willing to bet that the well-dressed woman gets smiled at more, people are eager to hold the door open for her and maybe even host longer conversations with her too. While on the other hand, the woman who doesn't appear to be as attractive gets passed by more on average and people, especially men, may not go out of their way to catch the door so that she can walk on through it with ease. Yes. It goes this way, and not because people are innately rude or dismissive. That's not it at all. People are, however, drawn to others who appear to take more pride in themselves. When you take the time to invest in your appearance, it communicates that you take yourself seriously so others should as well – and they do. Also, when you put yourself together with care, you perform better because you actually *feel* better. So, if you're not the kind of woman who has ever cared about her style for example, start now! Do whatever you can to develop a personal style that exudes femininity, beauty and confidence; and you will see how the world changes its response to you. If you are not sure where to begin, download a self-help app like "Pinterest", and search for a style that you believe resonates with you in order to achieve looks you can pull off for all occasions.

My personal advice? When it comes to work attire, you can't ever go wrong with a classy pair of nude or black 2' or 3' inch pumps, a sleek pencil skirt (not too tight), and a beautiful quality blouse. Throwing in a simple, timeless gold or two-tone watch is always a nice touch too. For romantic outings an "LBD", aka little black dress, that drops just above or below the knees has never steered me wrong either. So! If you are new to dressing up, but still want to feel sexy without overdoing it, you'll be in good shape if you go this route. Coupling your LBD with a simple evening bracelet and a nice pair of chandelier earrings would be even better. Just remember that classy instead of gaudy should always be your aim *especially* if you want your style to communicate your high value. If you actually invest in your wardrobe, you will have key pieces to play with for a *very* long time. Plus, quality just looks better and you will feel better in it. The better you feel, the better you'll perform remember?! The better you perform, the more the world opens up to you. When the world opens up to you, you feel a stronger connection to your femininity. Oh! Don't you dare forget your perfume- and make it a damn good one!

NOTES

NOTES

NOTES

NOTES

CHAPTER 17

Grab A Hold of Your Finances. Claim Your Joy!

Just thinking about how much my life changed when I started holding myself accountable for my finances excites me to share what I now know with you. I was fortunate enough to grow up middle class, but my father, who was also the primary breadwinner in our household, grew up very poor. Naturally, this made him work hard so that his wife and children could reap all of the benefits that he was not afforded as a child. I am, and have always been grateful for my father's hard work, but never wanting me to worry about money may have also been the reason that he neglected to teach me the importance of managing it. Being oblivious to how money actually worked was fine when I was a teenager living at home with no real responsibilities, but after my third year in college, I really started to feel the effects of my poor money comprehension skills. I kept telling myself that I would spend less and create a budget, but it was difficult to put this into practice because I always felt like money would just show up when I needed it. I worked in restaurants all throughout undergrad and post-bac premed, and the more I made the more I spent. One day, I started feeling depressed because I had worked consistently for years making great tips, but I had no money saved. Nothing. Rent was rising in my city, I was getting older, and my taste was becoming finer, but never having enough money started to make me anxious all of the time.

Today I am a successful real estate trader and my grip on my finances is much tighter. For the first year of my investing career however, I still had reckless habits and I was newly a six-figure earner. In the summer of 2017 between May and August, I made one-hundred fourteen thousand dollars in net gains, but by the end of that year I had pretty much blown it all. It hit me then that it was never about how much I was making, but it was all about my lack of financial education. There I was one week before Christmas, one-hundred thousand dollars less and ever more stressed. I knew that if I didn't get my act together, the amount of money I make wouldn't matter. I needed to actually learn about money and how to make it work for me.

You may have a similar story as mine or you might be naturally great with finances, but you still desire to make more money. Whatever your case is, I advise you to find and secure at least one additional source of income, other than that of your nine to five as quickly as you can. Why? Because I know first-hand how stressful it is and how disconnected a woman can feel from her femininity, when she is living in scarcity or worried over money *all* of the time. I know how difficult it is to wake up excited, ready to own the day when you are falling behind on bills. I know that hopeless feeling you get when you believe you are worthy of quality things such as nice shoes and bags, but just can't afford them; and it doesn't help that all day long social media highlights the most beautiful influencers who are wander lusting across the globe in their designer threads with seemingly no cares in the world. Believe me when I tell ya that I understand how hard it is to feel secure in yourself when everyone else seems to be doing many wonderful things, yet you only have just what you need to get by.

Becoming a real estate investor taught me something very important: there is money all around us and it can be yours if you open yourself up to making as much of it as you can. You do not have to be a slave to your desires if you work hard and keep your eyes and ears on the lookout for *opportunities*. I did this by first networking with other investors online via social apps like Facebook and LinkedIn. I'd always make it a point to connect with other investors and encourage them to keep me abreast of new opportunities both in and outside of the real estate world. Additionally, I joined my first mastermind in the Spring of 2019 which turned out to be the best twenty-five thousand dollars that I have invested to date. Not only did this mastermind provide me with really great systems which helped me scale my virtual real estate investment business, it also gave me access to more seasoned professionals who were already investing their money into other things from cash-flowing commercial assets to the e-comm market. Today, I no longer rely on my real estate investments alone. I have started coaching, writing, investing in the stock market, and digital education. I'm telling you this because learning the importance of placing my eggs in more than one basket propelled me to new heights. I now know that keeping money is one thing, but making even more of it by diversifying my earnings is just as necessary. Having the cushion of more than one stream of income will without a doubt make a difference in your life because you will actually be able to *enjoy* yourself more; and you'll feel so fabulous when you can actually afford the life that you want instead of spending your time being envious of others who are living the life that you wish to have for yourself.

Money *can* buy happiness, but it can't be the *only* thing that makes you happy. Still, you'll feel more secure about your life and all of the new possibilities in front of you when you have more money! Believe me. You will be able to move in more exclusive circles, dine out at finer establishments, travel the world in style and the list goes on. Taking control of your financial situation will open up many exciting doors! I don't even think that I can properly convey to you how beautiful life feels when your money problems are alleviated. The security that you will have! The joy that will radiate from within – a joy that others *won't be able to ignore.*

NOTES

NOTES

NOTES

NOTES

CHAPTER 18

Find Yourself in Feminine Company

Learning to become more feminine, or possibly even trying to reconnect to your femininity if you lost it somewhere along the way can feel overwhelming. You may find yourself wondering what femininity even looks like at this point in your life. You might not be so sure what feminine women like to do or how they stay in alignment with their feminine nature. I get it. While many women who are seeking really want to reclaim their femininity, they have very few tangible examples to model after. I hear things from my community that range from "my mother is in my life, but she is a tomboy" to "all of my friends are struggling with their femininity too and they don't even know it". Here's what I need you to do. Start being more intentional about networking with other really feminine women. From this day forward, you are not going to shy away from the vibrant, beautiful, and inspirational woman at your office or gym! You are going to talk to her! You are going to do the exact same thing when you're out and about and you see other women who radiate that feminine confidence that you admire. Yes! You read *all* of that right. I am actually asking you to put yourself "out there", but hey! You did say that you were willing to do whatever it takes which is why you have made it this far in the book anyway. I know that this will require some vulnerability on your part, which is essential to femininity anyway, but you will need to put your best foot forward by making every effort to find yourself in more feminine company if you *really* want to reclaim your femininity.

You are still reading which means that you are still breathing so that's good. Listen! Just think positive and stop being afraid to approach other women. I don't care what has happened in your past, it's time to kick the fear of rejection because you believe that you lack something. You lack nothing! You just haven't tapped into the *magic* that lies deep within you. The very next time you see a feminine woman who you holds your interest, get up the courage to approach her. As you are doing this, I quite literally want you to imagine the most positive outcome ever. Instead of thinking about all of the things that might go *wrong*, tell yourself that you are getting ready to make a new friend who is going to bring such an exciting perspective into your life and that approaching her can only go *right*! Just walk right up to her and say something like "Hi! You look so put together. How do you do that?" or maybe even "You really own the room when you walk in it. Where'd you learn that?". Smile and be as genuine as possible when you approach the girl and I am ninety-nine percent positive she will be so flattered that she'll tell you exactly what you need to know. You can also tell her that you are looking to connect with more feminine women and that you'd love for the two of you to keep in touch. It doesn't matter how you approach the situation, just make sure that you do!

Are you ready for some good news? Here it goes. We live in a digital world and just about anything that you are in search of can be found online. We have access to so much information that our mothers and grandmothers did not have so we can achieve any goal that we set out to achieve. Take it from someone who literally goes to Google and YouTube for everything! The other day I was trying to learn how to fire up a grille so I went right to my trusted friend YouTube! This may sound silly, but the same goes for "femininity". One of my favorite apps for connecting with people is called "meet ups" and it's very simple to use! You can create a membership for free and shortly after, you will be able to search for a community of people who share your interests. If you want to find golf buddies, go to meet ups. If you are looking for millennial professionals who love steak and wine, go to meet ups! If you want to find a community of women, just use meet ups! I would start by just searching for women groups in your area and see if anything that pops up interests you! I am certain that there is a group for girls in your city who are young, vibrant, and just looking to get out and network with other like-minded women! This is a great alternative for you if you are not too comfortable approaching the "it" girl at the office like I mentioned a bit earlier. Find out what these women are doing the next time you are free and go to "meet up" with them! There will be all kinds of women at this gathering so it'll be the perfect environment for you to study femininity, introduce yourself, and possibly build an organic relationship or two with someone who can show you how she uses *her* femininity to make the world her own!

Don't shy away from the more exclusive nail parlors, wax centers, and hair salons. Really feminine women love hanging out in nicer establishments such as these because they know that they'll be treated like high class ladies by the staff; and more than likely there will be other women hanging around who take pride in being just as well-groomed and beautiful as they do. Skip a few cocktails every month if this will help you save an extra thirty to forty dollars so that you can afford to frequent the higher-end venues. Remember! The goal is to find yourself in feminine company. You are going to be pleasantly surprised when you start intentionally moving in high value places and creating more feminine connections as a result. I remember when I first put myself on a wax schedule. Oh, yes. Every three and a half weeks without fail! Not only did getting on a schedule make me feel sexy and all grown up, but it also gave me the opportunity to meet some really great women. This was especially easy to do because like myself, most of the women who attended my wax parlor were on a schedule too! I felt like I was a part of an exclusive club that only feminine women knew about. We would all come to our appointments smelling really great, extremely well-dressed, make up done you name it. Going to my wax appointments was always a load of fun, but I was especially grateful that my eyes were opened to the value that moving in higher end, feminine spaces creates! My life was forever changed and I want the same thing for you!

Where you get your waxes, massages etc., may not seem important but your environments do matter now that you are on the journey to reclaiming your femininity. When you have some spare time this week, look into a new spa or nail salon and make sure that its high end. Rule of thumb?! Typically, those on the pricier side are. Take a look at their website, call them up and let the receptionist know that you're looking for a new place to get yourself pampered, but that you'd like to stop in for a tour first. It doesn't have to be a formal tour perse, but set the expectation that you're looking to do some due diligence before you give them your business. This is an especially classy way of not being pressured into actually purchasing a service if you can't yet afford to. When you go to your appointment, look great! Smell perfect and be as polite as possible. When you show up looking like someone special, you'll get special treatment even if you are just on a tour. Don't forget to really look around and take notice of the kind of women who are there. What do they look like? How do they carry themselves? Are they the type of women who you aspire to be like be or network with? Keep good mental notes and when your tour ends, either decide to schedule a service if you like what you saw or graciously thank the host for her time and then move on.

Whether you decide to stay or go, what's more important is that you got the opportunity to familiarize yourself with being in such an environment. If nothing else, take some time to reflect on what that meant to your femininity. I was reading a book on dating secrets from a male author not too long ago and he wrote something that really resonated with me. He said that being "cute" might get you some attention, but being gorgeous and "hot" definitely requires some extra effort, and it's this *extra* effort that sets you apart from other women. Feminine women understand that when you go the extra mile to take care of not just your insides, but your outward appearance too, you give off a unique energy. This energy signals to others that they believe they're worth the best and if they are going to make room for anyone and anything, then they have to be the very best as well. So! Do whatever it takes to start positioning yourself in places where high value feminine women hang out because being around them will keep you in the know about all things feminine. When you are in the know you can actually apply these things to your own life and I guarantee that you'll begin to see a major uptrend in who and what you attract; and when you feel good about what you are attracting into your life, you will feel that much more capable of reclaiming your femininity. Get around more feminine women now, and remember to be completely open to the newness of it all. *Doctor's orders!*

NOTES

NOTES

NOTES

NOTES

CHAPTER 19

Get Excited About Men!

---~∽⋒⋐~---

Men are wonderful. From Mars at times- definitely! Buuuut still great. Honestly though, could you really imagine a world without them? I can't, and I don't want to! Some women, however, act as if they do not like, trust, or enjoy men yet wonder why they are having trouble finding a good one. First and foremost, I am not overlooking the fact that men don't always apply the best care to women and that serious damage has been done to the feminine community as a result. I can't tell you how many times I have been on the receiving end of dishonesty or downright unattractive behavior from the men who I chose to entertain. This was of course before my taste in them matured. Notice that I did say, "men who I chose to entertain" though. In spite of how I may have felt about the outcome, *I* made the choice to be a part of every single relationship I was in. Accountability in dating and romance is a discussion that is worth having because before a certain level of maturity is reached, it can be easy to go through life believing that you are a victim. Sure, I have been disappointed by some of the men in my past, but rarely was I blind-sided. There was always a red flag that I ignored and usually very early on in the relationship. Each time that I took the warning signs for granted I was disappointed in the end. Pretending like I was the victim would've robbed me of the space to be honest with myself about the role I played in my own relationships.

Being soft, vulnerable, and gentle with men are not the reasons you have been hurt, or are currently in a less than ideal romantic situation. You aren't having the best luck in love because you refuse to trust your instincts. You dismiss valid gut feelings as paranoia and sometimes you fall for potential instead of what is in front of you. No judgement. I understand that women are lovers first and so it is natural to want to take others at their best. Still, I believe that the almighty God gave women a basic set of instincts to help balance out our natural and loving natures which sometimes makes us turn a blind eye to things that we know shouldn't. In spite of how difficult this can be at times, if you don't learn to lean into these instincts, you will have a harder time in romance.

Listen here's a little advice. If something feels off, it's because it is. There's no need to second-guess yourself or spend too much of your emotional equity on a completely unworthy investment. In this case, an unworthy man. Doing so can cause serious damage to your femininity and overtime, you'll start to feel negatively about all men.

There is good news. You do not need to be discouraged because high value men still exist! What exactly do I mean when I say high value? A high value man is someone who takes pride in being a *man*- a healthy, confident, and masculine man. He knows his "why" or has a strong sense of purpose. He has respect for himself and others and he does things in good character. He speaks with truth and kindness, keeps his word, has the admiration of his peers, community, and family members. He's confident in his sexuality. He knows the importance of leading, hunting, providing and the list goes on! Men like this are all around you, but you have got to exude warm and feminine energy to really be seen by and attract them. Men, and especially high-quality men can feel when a woman does not actually like, trust, or enjoy men. Because of who they are, they don't have any issues with getting women to be drawn to them so this means they have a ton of experience when it comes to dating and relationships. It's really hard to get much pass them so they can easily detect when they are in for a battle with a woman which they'll avoid at all costs. I am not saying that you need to be perfect nor pretend like you don't have any battle scars. What I am saying is that it's unfair to make a man pay for your past and can I be honest? No man who values his own sanity is going to.

Lighten up! Relax. Be joyful and leave the past where it belongs. In the daggon past. I can assure you that having a distasteful attitude will not win you any contests with men- at least not the *kind* of men who you will actually want to settle down with. We have all been through our fair share of disappointments so know that you are not alone. However, it's time to love in forward motion *and* get excited about men again. It's time to trust that not every guy is coming in your path all just to hurt you so forget that, and forget about those naysayers in your life who try to keep you believing in that. If your friends, aunties, or mom want to see the worst in men, let them! That is their choice. You, however, are on a beautiful feminine journey and your best days are waiting for the best version of you to show up. Even if you have to walk this road alone for a little while, decide right now that you are done believing the worst about men.

Thinking positively about men is really important, but this alone won't do you any good without a healthy set of boundaries to help you approach romance with dignity and direction. When a relationship is new it is really easy to lead with your feelings, but this can be dangerous. Think back on how many times you fell way too hard or way too fast because a guy was good looking and he said *all* the right things. Taking the time to actually write down some guidelines that you'll stick to throughout your dating life will help you quickly eliminate losers and time wasters so that you can be more easily found by ready men! Establishing healthy boundaries will also help keep you in check when the chemistry between you and a man is strong, for example, but the relationship is new and you might not be ready to take things to the next level until you're crystal clear on your feelings. When you are laying this list out for yourself, *always* keep in mind exactly what you want. Translation: DO NOT consider anything that you'd be willing to settle for if you start liking a man enough. Think of no one other than yourself, the kind of future that you know you deserve, and what it will realistically take to get you there. For example, knowing that you want marriage will help you create and stick to some winning boundaries. A few years ago, I decided that I was ready to be married so I needed to do what it would take to be a wife. I was also aware of the mistakes that I made in my past and how those mistakes kept me from being taken seriously in romance. Writing out a clear list so that I could finally date successfully was life-changing for me so I *definitely* recommend this to any woman who wants to be more successful in her love life as well.

You're probably wondering what was on my list right? Well! I'll tell you a little bit about it. Since I knew that marriage was the ultimate goal for me, I vowed to only take men seriously who wanted to be married too. I'd never pressure a man into telling me if he wanted to be married on the first date or anything, but I'd pay close attention to his actions to determine whether he was commitment-minded or not. Kissing was another healthy boundary on my list. I am a sensual person so I stopped allowing myself to kiss a man before he courted me properly enough to earn it. Kissing usually opens up the flood gates for other things and it can distract you before you have actually had the chance to assess whether a man has done right by you consistently. I also got intentional about asking questions in regards to past relationships. I neglected to do this before not realizing that patterns tell a story. You can learn a lot about what a man actually values by asking him questions about his past relationships. A man might say that he wants a long-term monogamous relationship for example, but has a history of infidelity. Usually, infidelity doesn't just stop because a man is with someone new so being aware of this early can help you determine if it's wise to get too deeply involved with him.

Obviously, there was much more to my list, but we would be here all day if I went through every bit of it. The goal of creating healthy and *realistic* boundaries is to understand what you want and to not waste time with a man who isn't right for you no matter how charming, sexy, or well-intentioned he is. Sure, you'll to meet men that you really like, but knowing what your boundaries are will keep you on track and equip you to make hard decisions when necessary. Let's say that you want children and a guy who you are really interested in tells you that he does not. If you already know that a man's decision to not have kids crosses a certain boundary of yours, then it'll be easier for you not to entertain him romantically. This decision won't be hard for you to make because you decided that motherhood is important to you *before* he came into the picture. You will be making a decision based on your goals instead of allowing yourself to be swayed in a different direction because you *like* the guy. Women who approach dating and romance fully aware of their boundaries usually have more success because they aren't easily sidetracked like those women who are not so clear on what they want or how they're going to get it. When you actually get what you want out of life because you stick to your values, you feel surer of yourself; and when a woman is more sure of herself, she naturally feels a deeper connection to her femininity.

NOTES

NOTES

NOTES

NOTES

CHAPTER 20

Only Take Men Seriously Who Are Willing to Court You

Netflix and chill? No deal. At least not before you have been courted first. Listen, men still date. They really do! I go out on dates very often and I see other couples out on dates too! This is a good thing because we are currently living in modern times and a culture exists that seems to influence dating in the opposite direction. In spite of this, mature commitment-minded men who believe in asking a woman out and getting to know her the right way still exists. You hear that ladies?! *Real* men who want to take you out on dates do still exist. No ifs ands or buts! I say this often and I'm going to keep saying it. There are some pretty significant ways to determine whether a man is into you. My top three include him taking you out on dates. Men love proving to the woman who they can see themselves with that they are capable of spending their hard-earned money on her. It's a part of the hunt for them and it makes them feel more "masculine". If he's not taking you out on proper dates, he isn't serious about getting to know you. Do not be naïve about this.

Never let a guy convince you that "he does not go on dates". He's testing you. The very same guy who claims he does not do dates or that he's a homebody, will be the exact same guy who you see out and about with another woman when you are enjoying a night in the city with your girls. Yup. This happens! Once I was into a guy. He was handsome, extremely sexy, successful and too many other things to name. I knew he wasn't "the one" for me, but I was still looking forward to getting to know him and learning more about myself through a mature romantic experience. I'll admit, knowing that he wasn't the one is part of the reason that I let certain things happen that I should have never let happen. One of these things was going over to his house too often early on in the relationship. As a result, a full year went by and we never went on a proper date. Our relationship consisted of house visits, great wine and food, and yes... sex. I was giving him access to one of my most prized possessions and the man never took me on a date. Yikes! Sounds absolutely ridiculous doesn't it? That's because it was. Wanna know what was even more ridiculous? Seeing him out on a lunch date one day with another woman. Yeeeup! You read that right. Here I am thinking that this guy doesn't do the whole public scene until he's exclusive with a woman, even though that's lazy too, only to find out that he was being casual with me the entire time. I wasn't hurt, but I was disappointed. In myself mostly. Thankfully, I was accompanied by a really handsome man that day, even though it was strictly professional. I was able to keep myself together like a lady and I paid him no mind when I caught him looking over at my table on more than one occasion. Eventually, he requested that he and his date's waiter find them another table inside which I actually thought was pretty hilarious.

I must say that seeing a man who I was spending so much time with on a date with another woman was a major blow. It was a weird situation to say the least because while we weren't in a committed relationship, there was so much intimacy and trust between us. I knew that he was capable of dating a woman the right way though. He had all of the means to do it so I wasn't surprised that he was out putting in the effort with *someone*. It still hurt to see a man who I had given so much of myself to doing something with another woman that he never took the initiative to do with me. Nope. Not one single time did he take me out on a proper date. I knew the insides of his bed, but not the insides of his car. What a funny thing indeed.

Saying that I allowed myself to get the short end of the stick would be an understatement and I felt sort of cheap too. Woman, if this sounds like you, it ends today! I don't care how good he looks and how smooth he talks, exposing yourself to situations like this will only cause you to second guess your own value, and if you are not careful, this will compromise your connection to your femininity over time. You do not want to look up six months from now and realize that the guy who you are dealing with never had any real intentions for you. If the relationship is new and he's asking you to "come over", it is in your best interest to politely decline- and keep on declining until he either gets the hint or goes away. If he steps his game up, wonderful! And hats off to you for putting your self-respect first. If he vanishes, that's good too because all you will have lost is someone who was just looking to waste your time. Etch this deep into your memory. If a man isn't making plans to take you out on dates, he's just not that serious about you.

Only take men seriously who will make sure that you understand through his words and his actions that you are adored. And you are certainly worthy of being treated with adoration. Adoration looks different for each woman so you will need to get clear on what makes you feel special if you are going to effectively communicate this to a man. A man may not come into a relationship knowing the specifics of what it is that you need, but if he is serious about you, he will learn what feels right for you. Remember that men love, love, love to earn what they see as special and they apply that same attitude to relationships with women.

NOTES

NOTES

NOTES

NOTES

FINAL THOUGHTS

It is my firm belief that every woman is born with an innate connection to her femininity and while it is every woman's birthright, this connection can be disrupted if it isn't cultivated properly- especially during the most primal years of life. On the other hand, some women are reared up to be extremely feminine, but after a series of let downs or failed romantic relationships, they themselves begin rejecting their femininity as a defense mechanism. No matter where you fall on the spectrum, I hope that this body of work has helped you understand *why* exactly reclaiming your femininity is so critical. Every woman has a special purpose whether she knows it yet or not, but fully tapping into that purpose can be challenging when a woman is operating outside of her nature; and when you aren't in the natural there's a lack of confidence and alignment. When you lack these things, you can't achieve true happiness and where there is no true happiness, there is no success. The world will never not need the woman and our femininity so do whatever it takes to get back to it! Work at it every day like your life depends on it because it does. You are here because you know that doing things your way hasn't been working. You can feel it which is why you came in search of new knowledge, and while I'm excited for you, the journey is just beginning.

Things are out of balance and there is work to be done in both the masculine *and* the feminine, but since we cannot control anyone other than ourselves, we must double down on doing our share. I believe that when women rise up, individually and collectively, we will witness a shift. I believe that this shift will be so divine and as a result, femininity and masculinity will exist in complete harmony again. In the interim please keep a few things in mind. The journey to reclaiming your femininity will take some dedication on your part, but the new woman that you'll become will make it all so worth it. Understand that every improvement, both big and small, is paying off even when it doesn't feel like it so don't forget to be patient with this journey and with yourself.

Finally, remember to be thankful. You may not always be celebrated for it, but it's so lady-like and commendable. Turn on the charm too! A woman who isn't afraid to use her feminine charm is attractive and she usually gets her way. So be effortless, alluring, and use your feminine charm. Also, yesterday was just that. Yesterday. Don't go overthinking or obsessing over what you could have done differently. There's always tomorrow! Actually, there's always today. And today is the perfect day to keep walking towards reclaiming your femininity. For good.

-*Doctor's orders*

Manufactured by Amazon.ca
Bolton, ON